GET INSIDE HER

THE FEMALE PERSPECTIVE

GET INSIDE HER
THE FEMALE PERSPECTIVE

Dirty Secrets from a Woman on
How to Attract,
Seduce, and
Get Any Female You Want

Marni Kinrys

THE ULTIMATE WING GIRL

Edited by Rebecca McLeod

Velocity House Publishing

ISBN: 978-1624090127

Dedication

I thank every person I have ever encountered who made me feel anxious. Each of those people pushed my buttons and frustrated me at the time, but ultimately these encounters pushed me to become the woman I am today.

I dedicate this book to:

Justine Mazin for her incredible, funny chapter introductions.

All the men who have supported the Wing Girl Method and me for the past decade.

The ex-boyfriends that hurt or loved me.

My amazing male friends.

My kick-ass girlfriends who have allowed me to interrogate them for intimate details and strap microphones to their bodies so I could complete my research.

My family, for supporting me and my ideas no matter how crazy they seemed

The best man among all men, my husband. Without him I would not have an example of what it truly means to be a man that women want! He is a man who I hope to spend the rest of my life with.

Special thanks to my industry peeps: everyone in The Seduction Syndicate, Sean Stephenson, Eben Pagen, Carlos Xuma, David Wygant, Josh Pellicer, Mark Ling, Nina Rubin, Neil Strauss, Ross Jefferies, Nicole Powers, Brian Gross, Kelly Perkins, and Rabbi Shwartzie.

Table of Contents

Preface 1

Introduction 3

How to Use This Book 13

I. What the F do Women Want? 14

  1. What They Definitely Don't Want 15

    Do Women Really Prefer Bad Boys to Nice Guys? ... 15

    Women Do Not Want to Be With the Bad Boy! 15

    Why Men Give Bad Advice 17

    Too Much Game Can Ruin Your Chances with Women 19

    Angry, Bitter Men Do Not Get Laid 26

    No Woman Likes a Pouncer 28

    Do Money, Social Status, and Possessions Matter To Women? 30

    Why Do Women Respond to Me When I Act Like an Asshole? 31

    Do I Need To Be Funny To Get The Girl? 32

    Is It Wrong To Date Women You Know You Do Not Want? 34

    How Long Should I Keep Up The Game? 35

  2. Surprise! The Things They Do Want. 36

The Short, Bald Man That Turned Me On 36

Do You Have The Presence Women Want?............40

You Must Turn Yourself on Before You Can Turn a
Woman On 42

Why Confidence Is More Attractive Than a Six-Pack
and Cash..43

Four Things You Need To Do To Get Women 47

Three Things Women Find Sexy That Have Nothing to
Do With Sex...48

Real Men Take Risks...50

Rules for Attracting Beautiful Women....................52

Women Want a Strong Man 55

Why Women Like 50 Shades of Grey 62

II.   How to Approach and Meet Women 66

  1.   The Where and How: 68

Where to Meet Women..68

How to Meet Women While Travelling 71

When Should A Guy Approach A Woman?.............73

Get Off Your Ass and Start Practicing! 75

Does Practice Really Get Results?............................76

Is She Testing Me? 78

How Do I Handle Female Cock Blocks? 79

How Do I Build Attraction and Take It to the Next
Level? 81

2. Body Language and Headspace 84

How to Show Confident Body Language When
Approaching Women 84

Nine Tips for Confident Body Language...................84

A Smile Is an Inexpensive Way to Change Your Looks
....88

Is the Initial Smile Essential? 91

25 Famous Thinkers and Their Inspiring Daily Rituals
....93

Reject Me Please!...102

How Do I Motivate Myself to Go for It When I Know
I'll Get Rejected? 104

Five Steps to Eliminate Approach Anxiety 105

How Can I Tell What a Woman's Eye Contact is
Signaling? 107

Are You Into This Girl? 109

How to Avoid Being Creepy 110

3. Dating Online 113

How to Write a Female-Friendly Profile 113

Rules for Selecting Pictures....................................119

Things to Include In Your Profile 120

How Do I Ask Her Out On Facebook?.....................122

III. How to Talk to Women and Create Attraction 124

Have You Heard About the Magic Line to Say to Women That Instantly Makes Them Drop Their Panties? 125

What Do I Talk to Women About? 125

Talking About Video Games 127

How to Compliment a Woman Correctly 128

Get Out Of Interview Mode and Start Connecting 131

Why Women Need to Feel You 134

How Do You Make Women Feel You? 136

How to Make Decisions in 60 Seconds Or Less 138

How to Get a Girl's Number in Less Than 30 Seconds 141

IV.   The Dating Playbook 147

Why Isn't Dating Fun Anymore? 147

1.   How to Get a Date 150

A Case Study: How to Correctly Ask a Woman Out 150

How to Be Direct and Ask Her Out 155

Are You Coming On Too Strong? How to Avoid Being Overeager 157

Do I Need to Have a Full Conversation With a Woman Before Asking Her Out? 161

How Do I Ask a Woman On a Second Date? 162

Is Okay to Date on a Casual Level? 163

Do I Tell a Woman I'm Dating Other Women? 165

2. How to Rock the Date 166

Eleven Mistakes Men Make on Dates....................166

Where to Take a Girl on a Date..............................170

How to Bring Up Sticky Topics: Kids, Divorce, Health, etc..171

Should Men Pay for the First Date? 174

How Can I Tell if She Likes Me?..............................179

Signs That She Wants to Be Kissed & Signs That She Doesn't..181

What Should I Do When A Woman Flakes On Me? 185

Did I Ruin My Chances by Getting Too Cute Too Soon?...188

Should I Call or Text after a Date? 189

Ten Reasons Why Being Unhealthy Can Affect Your Dating Life 191

V. How to Avoid the Friend Zone 195

Urban Legend: The Man Who Went From Friend to Lover Just by Waiting 195

The Difference Between a Friend and a Lover.......196

Do I Stay in the Friend Zone and Wait? 199

Have I Become "The Friend"? If So, How Do I Escape the Friend Zone? 201

How to Be a Bad Friend but a Freaking Good Lover 204

She's Just Not That Into You: Don't Mistake Emotional Banter for Flirtatious Banter 230

What Do I Do If She Starts Talking About Her Guy Problems on a Date? 232

She Brought Her Ex on Our Date 233

VI.   How Women Want It! The How, What, Where, When and Why Behind Every Female Action. 235

Eleven Things about Beautiful Women Every Man Must Know 235

What Do Women Find Sexy? 240

Do Women Want Sex As Much As Men Do? 243

Ten Ways to Get Her in the Mood 246

Eight Signs That She Is Flirting with You 249

The Three Magic Words Every Woman Wants To Hear 252

How to Be Her Hero 255

How to Win Over a Bitch 258

Why Do Women Flake on Plans? 260

Why Do Women "Test" Men: The Shit Test Explained 264

How to Pass Shit Tests 268

Is She A Gold Digger? 269

How Do I Breakup with A Girl and Still Be Friends? 271

How Do Women Evaluate the Men Who Approach Them? 273

Why Do Women Give Out Their Number & Not Answer the Phone? 274

What Does It Mean When a Women Says "You Don't Listen Unless I Yell?" 276

VII.   Conclusion..278

The Checklist 278

The Formula for Success 280

The Happily Ever After 282

VIII.   References 286

Preface

I have been trying to write this book for four years. By trying I mean attempting to pawn off the work on someone else who I thought could more creatively present the work I've been doing for nearly a decade.

Every time I tried, the writer failed to convey what I wanted. The content of the book didn't convey the passion I have for my life's work. I wanted perfection. I wanted everyone to love what I wrote and I wanted every guy who picked up a book with my name on it to be magically motivated and transformed.

Then I realized something...

I was doing exactly what I tell men, every day, to stop doing. I was stopping myself from going after what I wanted because I was afraid of failure. Just as you cannot attract and charm the pants off every woman, you cannot create the perfect book that will motivate and transform every man.

So I said, "Fuck it," and started putting together my book! My advice has already helped hundreds of thousands of men around the world. A little poor grammar and shoddy spelling were not going to hold me back. This book represents close to a decade of hard work, constant testing, as well as years of being in the trenches with clients and friends.

This book is a compilation of the work I have been doing for almost a decade. I've gathered what I think to be my best blogs, articles, newsletters, emails to clients, stories, and

To access FREE bonus materials go to:
http://winggirldatingtips.com/gih-bonuses/

responses to comments on my website and I have put them all into one place.

This book is not designed to make you feel good about the things you have done in the past. Men come to my website, sign up for my programs and buy my books because they want a female perspective. I make it my goal to give them that perspective, and sometimes it hurts.

It can be hard to hear that you've been going about getting a date in totally the wrong way, but it can stop right now. As a woman who studies what women want, I am going to tell you exactly how to approach women.

You are going to learn in-depth, real things about women; the things they want, the things they expect, and why what you are doing now and have been doing until now is not working. The pieces I have gathered for you do not tell you how women should act; they tell you how they do act.

Enjoy.

The Last Female Friend You'll Ever Need, Marni

Introduction

I waited backstage at the Renaissance Hotel ballroom, where the Pick-Up Artist Summit was in full swing and I was the next scheduled speaker. If you are not familiar with the term Pick-Up Artist, it means a man (generally) who is skilled at meeting, attracting, and seducing women.

Typically, Pick-Up Artists, or PUAs, are associated with the seduction community, a heterosexual male subculture based on the goal of improved sexual and romantic abilities with women. For years this world has been kept a secret but with the success of VH1's show "The Pick Up Artist" and Neil Strauss' bestselling book "The Game" (Strauss, 2005), it's not so secret anymore. In fact, it has become a big business.

The PUA Summit is a gathering of the world's top PUAs and their followers who are eager to learn. Some of the experts teach pick-up lines, while others teach routines, but all teach their method on the art of getting the girl. If you're confused as to why I, a woman, was speaking at the PUA Summit, let me give a quick description of my job: I pick up women for men.

My name is Marni and I am a professional Wing Girl.

Men pay me to help them pick-up, attract, date, and get the women they want. Not to brag, but I'm really freaking good at it. Besides being invited to speak at the PUA Summit this year where I was awarded, "World's Best Female PUA of

To access FREE bonus materials go to:
http://winggirldatingtips.com/gih-bonuses/

the Year," I have successfully helped thousands of great men get the women they want.

So how did a nice Jewish girl like me get into this profession? I started my business, the same way most people do: drunk and by accident.

One Friday night, I attended a Shabbat dinner at the home of Rabbi Shwartzie. I am not religious but I was new to Los Angeles and wanted to connect with my people. Just like any other Jewish event, this dinner was also a singles mixer. I had recently started dating someone (who I am now married to) but felt there was no harm in window-shopping.

The matching making soiree was off to a rocky start, and the event felt more like a junior high dance than a singles mixer. Boys on one side of the room, girls on the other side. No one was interacting. I started grabbing men and pushing them to talk to women. When they were finished interacting, I would give them feedback on their technique, made tweaks and send them out again. By the end of the night, people were mixing, exchanging numbers, and having a great time.

I went home, buzzed from the night and the open bar, and spoke to my roommate. I was in public relations at the time and hated every second of it. I said to him, "What if I could do what I did tonight, but as a job? What if I was a professional Wing Girl"? My roommate responded with, "There's no way guys would pay for a service like that unless you threw in a BJ and case of beer." I disagreed, marched into my bedroom, and put an ad up on Craigslist. It went something like this: "What better way to attract bees than with honey? All you have to do is sit back, relax and I'll bring the women to you..."

By the next morning, I had over 75 responses and the start of a brand new business! I have to admit; the first few months were somewhat frustrating because I was trying to figure out exactly what it was that I had created. The media pounced on me, men were intrigued, a pimp even wanted me to join his ring, and of course, my family was concerned. I had no idea what I was doing, but I didn't let that stop me.

I took The Wing Girl Method to a completely new level when I met a man named David DeAngelo. David invited me to speak at one of his PUA events called "Mastering the Art of Approaching Women ("The art of," 2010)." What I didn't know about David at that time (real name Eben Pagen) was that he was a master online marketer and he was filming his seminar so he could distribute DVDs to hundreds of thousands of men around the world.

That is how I found myself quickly pushed into the world of Pick-Up artistry and became the first female run and operated business in the industry dedicated to helping great guys date beautiful women. All of a sudden, I was recognized at Starbucks by men who had seen the David DeAngelo DVD and was getting requests from every top PUA around the world to interview me for my unique female perspective.

Since then, I have spent the last decade helping tens of thousands of men around the world go from being Mr. Nice Guy to Mr. Holy Shit, I Want Him!

Now I am going to do the same for you.

It's no secret that women are hard to understand. You can never be sure what will turn us on, turn us off, or arouse our fury. In addition, you do not know what we say when guys

To access FREE bonus materials go to:
http://winggirldatingtips.com/gih-bonuses/

are not around. It is easy to feel lost trying to attract and date women and make sense of their behavior. I know how confusing the feminine nature can be.

Imagine how easy your life would be if you understood women as well as you understand so many other things! With my help, you will not have to imagine anymore! From here on out, you can refer to me as your very own Wing Girl! I am going to peel back the layers of mystery and reveal to you the secrets of female nature.

That means I will do what your older sister or your best female friend should have done a long time ago: tell you everything you need to know about what you need to be, what you need to do, and what you need to change in order to attract and date the women you want.

However, before we go any further, I want to make one thing clear to you: I am not a pick-up artist! Even though it is where I got my start, I do not consider myself a Pick-Up Artist. I do not teach routines, pick-up lines or any type of romantic manipulation. In fact, I believe that much of the top Pick-Up Artist material actually does more harm than help.

Why?

Because many pick-up techniques stress the goal of feeling superior to women in order to gain success with women. This creates an unequal dynamic causing insecurity to be the driving force behind a woman's attraction. This is unhelpful because the attraction is not real and the insecurity will manifest itself later in the form of incessant testing and resistance to physical escalation. I have seen men develop "approach anxiety" and lose confidence trying to use the techniques recommended by so-called gurus (who do not understand women). In fact, I believe this is one of the primary reasons that men have trouble attracting women. They are listening to so-called pick-up gurus. These "systems" actually end up turning men into anxious teenage girls, always wondering if what they are doing is right and becoming nervous and uncollected.

The Wing Girl Method is clear, it's simple, it's intuitive, and it's easy to put into practice. I am not going to bog you down with jargon or fancy words so that you go along with something that you know makes no sense in order to strip you of your money. I am going to give you the facts. My goal is not to transform you into a robotic machine that repeats the same phrases until it is taught a new killer routine, but to help women appreciate you for the great guy I know you are!

I am going to give you the skill-sets that allow you to carry on a regular conversation and actually relate to the woman you are talking to rather than simply throwing up a routine on her. These skill-sets stay with you at all times and make it so simple that you can adapt them to any situation and deal with any obstacle calmly and coolly.

The materials I provide will show you how to boost your sexual and masculine confidence by gaining a clearer understanding of how women work, what they want, and why they do the things they do. This strong masculine presence will allow you to attract women.

I know what you are thinking... "She doesn't understand."

To access FREE bonus materials go to:
http://winggirldatingtips.com/gih-bonuses/

I wish I could say that was true, but for years I struggled like you -unsure of myself, I suffered from severe social anxiety, and was constantly living in my head. It took a tremendous wakeup call - one that put my life in danger - to start making real changes in how I approached other people. It reached a point of such severity that when I was only twenty-years old I had a stroke.

To say it was one of the most stressful years of my life would be an immense understatement. After following a man to a college, only to break up with him a month later, disconnecting from all of my friends and struggling with an eating disorder for most of a year, my body hit a barrier. While working as a summer camp counselor, I collapsed. When I awoke, I was partially paralyzed. I could barely communicate with those around me.

From there, things just got worse. It did not matter that I had bleeding in my brain that resulted in a minor stroke. The side effects created a deep state of self-consciousness than I had never felt before. I was harshly judging myself, which created a barrier between others and me.

I was lonely, frustrated, and lost. It took almost two years to recover.

At the age of 23, after school, I decided to make a change and moved to Los Angeles. On the day I left, I made a huge promise to myself. I told myself, "I'm going to break free of the judgments I place on myself. I'm going to try new things. I'm going to meet new people and break down these barriers that are stopping me from connecting to others."

When I got to Los Angeles, I dove head first into pushing myself to do things that I was otherwise afraid of doing. The move to Los Angeles had been the biggest risk I ever taken; why not take just one more? I decided to go dancing despite my injury, which had made dancing nearly impossible without feeling self-conscious. I met new and interesting people who were not like me but that was okay. I created a new life for myself and I did it through the greatest adversity I had ever felt.

So now you are probably thinking, all right she gets me a little bit more, but how is a woman going to help me gain a strong masculine character?

I'll tell you.

Belief: Women give bad advice to men about what women want.

Truth: Most women give bad advice to men about what women want.

Many women do not actually understand what they want or why they do the things they do. Most women will be able to tell you exactly what they wish they wanted, but very few are able to say what they genuinely want or need from a man. In fact, I recently put out an ad asking for women with opinions on what women want from men. I received over 600 responses from women around the world.

Beautiful, intelligent women who I later discovered had absolutely no idea what it was they wanted, what they were attracted to or what they responded to when filling in the answers. I was shocked. However, one thing I did learn is that women are very interested in being heard. Save that note for later!

For some women, it is difficult to admit to some of the behaviors they respond to. This is either because they are embarrassed or because they really do not have a clue but desperately want to figure it out. I also found that most women place themselves on a social pedestal and are fearful of falling off.

I have always known many guys growing up and often saw things from their perspective. I have winced at how they misinterpreted women. I saw firsthand the key places where woman miscommunicated to men and where men failed to understand the signals women were sending. I have come to understand what both sides mean when they try to express what they want and I have experienced the misunderstanding myself and saw how destructive it can be to happiness.

I have been attracted to men. I have loved men, hated men, and been hurt by men. I have gotten revenge on men, felt insecure with men, and had sex with men. I have led men on, flirted with men for fun, and taken great pleasure in teasing men. I have broken up with men for no reason. I have avoided men, flaked on men, given out my number with no intention of answering the phone. I have had one-night stands with men. I have been in long-term relationships with men. I have even placed men in the Friend Zone when I knew they deserved a romantic chance. I have experienced every scenario you have possibly experienced, but on the other side.

With my help, you are going to become the guy who understands the subtle communication that occurs between men and women. You will be able to attract women because you'll understand what women want to communicate. These women will be attracted to you, not your money or possessions, but who you are and how you can make them feel.

Here's just a little of what I am going to teach you:

- What women are really looking for

- What do women really mean when they say certain things

- How women evaluate men

- How you can fine tune your approach

- How you can avoid the mistakes that most men make

- Why looks don't matter to women

- How women can sense a man's presence and intention

- Why saying the right thing doesn't work

- The definite signs that she likes you and what to do next

- How to escalate sexually with women without getting slapped

This is just the start.

With me as your personal Wing Girl, you will hone an approach that is unique to you. You will become a great communicator. You will understand how to please a woman

To access FREE bonus materials go to:
http://winggirldatingtips.com/gih-bonuses/

both emotionally and sexually. You will become a man that women want. You will also become the man you have always wanted to be.

How to Use This Book

This book was written to provide advice on a variety of topics, all for understanding my crazy gender. What I hope you learn from this book is that women are not the enemy and that they are not mythical, magical creatures with breasts, best-suited for a pedestal. They are good, decent, loving people, just like you.

This book can be read in small chunks for when you need specific advice. You can also dive straight in and read the book cover to cover. The most important thing is that you read with an open mind and understand that what I share with you may not be the most appealing picture of women you will ever see. However, it is the most accurate.

There are little surprises sprinkled throughout the book - you may want to go back through if you skip over anything to make sure you catch those!

To access these special bonuses, along with some surprises from me, go to:

http://www.winggirlmethod.com/get-insider-her-bonus

Enough chitchat, let's get started!

To access FREE bonus materials go to:
http://winggirldatingtips.com/gih-bonuses/

I. What the F do Women Want?

Do not be timid or tentative. A man who is self-assured and assertive will touch in a casual manner, without hesitancy or uncertainty.
—CLAIRE, 32

There are many clichés about finding love. "You will know it when you see it." "When you know, you know." "It will feel different from anything you have ever felt." These are all very mystical notions. They are also very aggravating. The idea of knowing or feeling indicates that there's a higher power involved, that this kind of attraction is based on chemistry, on planets and signs, on destiny -- what you do or say has nothing to do with it. Women are usually the ones who use these clichés, and they use them with goofy grins painted across their faces. "I just knew." "I had butterflies." "It can happen to you too." As your Wing Girl, I will let you in on a little secret: Love is not as cosmically determined as women would like to believe.

There is a recipe for creating butterflies, and I am going to give it to you.

1. What They Definitely Don't Want

Do Women Really Prefer Bad Boys to Nice Guys?

Many men believe women want to be with the Bad Boy and that being labeled as "Nice" is the kiss of death. The first thing that I want to get out there is that women *do* want to be with a nice man; what they do not want is a man who is a wimp. There is a big difference. "Nice" is simply the polite term women use when what they really mean is "Grow some freaking balls and stop being a wimp!"

Women Do Not Want to Be With the Bad Boy!

I have never heard of a woman sitting with her friends during Girls' Night who said, "I can't wait until I meet a jerk who will treat me poorly, belittle me on a daily basis, and show absolutely no respect for me." If that is what you believe women want. . .we have some serious work to do!

I will admit that I understand how this rumor started and why so many men still believe that acting like a jerk will get them everything they want with women. Every day you see women with guys who you know don't deserve them; jerks or downright douche bags with amazing women by their sides.

To access FREE bonus materials go to:
http://winggirldatingtips.com/gih-bonuses/

You may even be the shoulder that those women cry on when these guys act like selfish scumbags. You think to yourself, "I'm a great guy; I should be with this girl. I have to become just like those jerks so that girls will date me." Let me explain why these women keep going back to those Bad Boy characters.

Sadly, the Bad Boys are the ones who approach women. Nice Guys rarely approach women and if they do, they screw it up every time because they instantly put the woman on a pedestal. Bad Boys are confident in themselves, respect the lives they have created, and they go after the women they want without fear of rejection. In the beginning, they display characteristics of a man any girl would want to be with. They show confidence, self-respect, independence, leadership, passion, and desirability to other women. Then something interesting happens. Slowly their true colors start to show and it becomes apparent that they are jerks.

However, by this point a woman is hooked on the Bad Boy. She believes that her first evaluation of him was correct and is embarrassed by her seeming "stupidity." She tries to change him back into that great guy that she believes he secretly is. She tries to make him into a man he will never be. And so the vicious cycle begins. It continues until she is finally ready to give up and cut her losses. This can take a long time.

I see it happen constantly with my female friends. I hear them complain, get mad, and try everything to turn their Bad Boy into the Nice Guy they thought he was, and that they demand he be. I can tell you for a fact that women do not want to be with Bad Boys, Jerks, and assholes. Who would?

What we do want is a mix of the Knight in Shining Armor who sweeps us off our feet and the Bad Biker Boy from the wrong side of the tracks who takes us on a thrill ride. A woman wants a man with a backbone, one who will tell her when she is wrong. She wants a man who will not lie down and play dead when she is being overly demanding or bossy.

A strong, independent woman wants a man who will treat her well. She will not go searching for a "player" or a two-timing douche-bag. All we are asking for is a man to treat us with respect yet at the same time respect himself. Women do not want to be with a Bad Boy. What women want is to be with a Nice Guy that is confident and a leader; who holds boundaries, and respects himself. A Nice Guy with all the Bad Boy strengths. In my eyes, Nice Guys will always have massive sex appeal!

Why Men Give Bad Advice

Just when I think, I have taken men two steps forward, I get emails like the one following. Emails from guys telling me they have stumbled upon Pick-Up Artist materials or advice from a "reputable resource" that their friends recommend. Inevitably, it blows up in their faces. Check out the email on the next page from a guy who stumbled upon an old Tom Leykis segment and was given the typical advice of "just treat girls like crap." Also, check out how the tactic blew up in his face!

From: ███████

Subject: **Re: VIP Email Support**

Date: November 27, 2011 9:17:10 PM PST

To: Marni (Your Wing Girl) <VIP@winggirlmethod.com>

By the way, when you have some free time, I have a dating story from today that I think you'll find quite amusing.

I was on youtube this afternoon and ran across a video from Tom Leykis giving his advice on dating. After one video, I was hooked and watched like 10 of them. He said not to be nice to a girl and instead treat her like crap, be completely unreliable, spend as little money on her as possible, and, in return, she'll be very attracted to you. People have told me in the past to be a gentleman with women and it's yielded poor results - women have played games and showed no interest in return, I'm out a lot of money, and I feel like the whipped sucker. So, I figured it would be worth trying Tom's advice out.

I had a match.com dinner date set up with a girl for this evening so it was the perfect chance. I honestly just wanted to go out for drinks, but, when we talked on the phone she had insisted on setting it up at dinner time so I initially set it as dinner.. Then, per Tom's advice, I texted her about 2 hours before the date and pushed it out an hour and switched it to drinks. I figured that would 'treat her like crap' and make me unreliable in her eyes.

Needless to say, it didn't work. She texted me an hour later and said she wasn't interested in meeting anymore. Luckily for me, I wasn't that interested in her (which is why she was a good test subject). After a couple of text exchanges she seems to have calmed down and said she's looking for a special person and doesn't want more friends and what I did turned her off. She said she's going to call me later to talk (it should be a fun conversation :).

I sure hope your advice works better Marni!! I think Tom set a pretty low bar ;-)

███████

My reply:

On Mon, Nov 28, 2011 at 5:18 PM, Marni (Your Wing Girl) <VIP@winggirlmethod.com> wrote:

OH dear!! Tom Lykis is off the air for a reason ;-) He was an ANGRY, frustrated man. BUT he did have a few great things to say. I will give hm that.

Just to be clear NEVER treat a woman like crap. Would you ever want a person treating you like crap?? No. On the flip side, never use Nice Guy Manipulation on a woman. Meaning, don't be a wimpy suck with a woman and allow her to walk all over you. Equally as insulting as treating a woman like crap.

I believe in a balance of being a great guy who has boundaries, respects himself and is open to listening and compromise.

For example - a woman suggests a place for a first date. You can be a wimp and say OK. Silently saying OK you take the lead. I'll just leave my balls in the corner. Or better yet I can just give them to you.

Or you can say - that's a great suggestion. I know the perfect place to go for a drink before. It's just around the corner. Let's meet at X at 7 and then if we want, we can head over to Y for a drink?

See how you can be a good guy AND still be a leader who makes decisions without being a dick!

Please do not listen to anyone who tells you that women are attracted to men who treat them like crap. The women who are drawn to this type of abuse are highly insecure and come with tons of baggage. Trust me, you do not want to deal with that.

Too Much Game Can Ruin Your Chances with Women

Many men get carried away trying to play "The Game"--so carried away with being charming that they lose the girl! Listen, I am the first one to admit that I love the game! I love the banter, the butterflies, the teasing, all of it. It is fun, but only for a night, maybe two at the most. After that, I need something a little more substantial or I'll move on.

A while back when I was first introduced to the world of the Pick-Up Artists, I met one of its leaders, Mystery, while speaking at a David DeAngelo seminar. In case you do not know what a Pick-Up Artist is, I will explain. A Pick-Up Artist is a man who considers himself skilled (or who tries to be skilled) at meeting, attracting, and seducing women. The term Pick-Up Artist is associated with the seduction community which is a heterosexual male subculture based on the goal of improved sexual and romantic abilities with women. Pick-Up Artists develop pick-up lines, routines, and gambits. They aim to improve their seductive capabilities through the development of different lifestyles. Many Pick-Up Artists use manipulative tactics to feed off a woman's insecurities, seduce her, and get what they want. These techniques not only hurt women but also men. The more women interact with a said "Pick-Up Artists" and get hurt, the more cautious they will be with all men. This means higher hurdles for regular guys to jump over.

Back to my point. . .I met Mystery. He was a tall man wearing a top hat, nail polish and a leotard. I kid you not. He introduced himself by teasing me and telling me stories, which honestly kept me captivated for an hour. I understand how his game works, and it worked on me. I was excited, bubbly, and dying for him to want me. Did I want him? Not at all, but I wanted him to want me. Do you see the difference?

I did not fall madly in love with him, nor did I think we had a great connection, but I had an urge for him to like me and want me. Once we separated, though, I did not think of him again. I didn't want to talk to him the next day or for him to call me. I got everything out of him that I wanted. I knew there was nothing else he could offer. His magic only worked for a short period of time because I had nothing real to feel connected to. I was simply entertained.

Many of the men that I work with on a daily basis are or have been part of the Pick-Up Artist community. They have consumed tons of Pick-Up Artist materials and have probably done a boot camp or two with a top Pick-Up Artist. These men have no problem engaging and approaching women, but they all come to me with the same problem.

"Where did I go wrong? How did I lose her?"

The answer to those questions is that they were so wrapped up in the game that they forgot to be present and connect to the woman in front of them. They have learned to capture an audience but they have not learned how to make that audience want more. At the core, most Pick-Up Artist programs mean well. However, if used incorrectly, they do a lot more harm than good.

These programs fall short because they dehumanize men and women alike, making it nearly impossible to form a real connection. I am going to give you a straight and honest female perspective. As a man, you have to give women a little more than entertainment to win her heart. I receive many of these emails, but I just want to share a few with you that show the kinds of mistakes men tend to make when they take the wrong advice.

The following email is from a 26-year-old man in London, England.

Hey Marni,

Wanted to ask you a question but I am going to need to explain the situation to you first so you get the full picture. It was a singles' social boat-cruise, and the following are the events that happened with one of the cuties that I am interested in dating. Need some opinion on how to pick up the momentum.

The particular cutie that caught my eye I approached by grabbing her by her arm and telling her to follow me. She came along willingly.

Me: Why were you avoiding me all night?

Her: I was not; you were busy running around with other girls.

Me: Wait, are you single?

Her: Yes, of course

Me: You had better be, otherwise I would have to kick you off the boat!

Her: *Dead air*

Me: Are you a good girl or a nice girl?

Her: Naughty but nice.

Me: Do you speak English?

Her: Yes.

Me: Choose one then...good or nice?

Her: Nice I guess.

Me. Do you know the difference?

Her: You tell me.

Me: Good Girl goes out, comes home and sleeps; Nice Girl goes out, sleeps and comes home.

*Her: *Dead air**

Me: Do you know the difference between Good Secretary and a Nice Secretary?

Her: No, go ahead.

Me: Good Secretary will say, "Good morning, Sir," and Nice Secretary will say, "It's morning, Sir."

*Her: *Dead air**

Then we have a chat about where she is staying, her ethnic mix, and places she has traveled. She turns out to be Singaporean and British.

Me: I bet you suck at Thumb-Wrestling!"

Her: Bring it on.

Me: I do not play without a wager.

Her: What is the wager?

Me: Loser buys dinner. Her: Okay.

Me: No Cheating! Best out of three, go!

Last round, I start to tickle her and wrestle with her. It is good fun with some tension. I lose on purpose because I tickled her. I say, "Okay, give me your number and we'll set something up." We part. The next hour, we exchange glances and I throw a few "I'm watching you" and "Stay out of trouble" lines at her, at which she giggles (most probably from a nice dosage of alcohol).

Friday: Cool off.

Saturday: Message her to check if she got home alive and ask for her email address. She replies okay and gives me her email address.

Sunday Morning: Call and leave a message. She calls back and we have a chat about setting a date, but we both have commitments. She mentions briefly to be in contact next weekend if we can do something together. I say, "Okay, we'll see."

I then ask her what she is doing. It's almost noon, why is she lazing like a pig? She giggles and says she has plans with some friends to watch Sex and the City.

Me: So which character best describe you?

Her: I don't know, what do you think?

Me: I think you are a Samantha in Charlotte disguise.

To access FREE bonus materials go to:
http://winggirldatingtips.com/gih-bonuses/

Her: No, no one likes to be her. It's not nice.

Me: Are you judging her? You are even more evil.

Her: No.

Me: I must go, got training, will call and catch up.

I text her later telling her I had to cut her short because I was dealing with London traffic. Will call at night to catch up and have some stimulating conversations. End with Charlotte and a wink. I called her at 10:30 pm, went to her voice mail. I say, "Ah, playing hard to get? Cheeky! Holler back!" I have not heard from her since.

Tuesday 11 pm, sent her a funny text: "It's important to find a man who has money, a man who adores you, and a man who is great in the sack. It is also important that these three men should never meet! How are you doing?" Did not receive any reply.

Any opinion as to how I can pick my game up again?

My response to the email:

What I noticed from your email is that you need to stop playing games. Games like this are fun in the moment. They are entertaining and get a girl's heart racing, but once this moment passes, reality sets in and girls realize what this behavior really means. It means games and sex with no phone call the next day.

You had her in your first interaction, and to be honest, if you had initiated taking it to the next level (bedroom, kiss, whatever), most likely she would have played ball. However, you stretched it out with her and therefore the endless banter became tiresome and dull. One thing I want to point out to you was the Sex and the City joke.

First, I was impressed that you know the characters. That's a start.

Second, no woman wants to be referred to as a Samantha by a man who is trying to sleep with her. If you call a girl Samantha, you are telling her "You're slutty and I think you're easy." Even if it is true, no woman wants to hear that. That little statement will have her feeling that there is only one thing on your mind.

Women want to be in control of their own sexuality and know they are respected even if they are sexually adventurous and open. Do not pigeon-hole women by telling them who they are; let them tell you who they are.

You will get much more out of a woman that way. Always give a woman something she can latch onto. Something she can hold onto that makes her feel that there is more to this than games, banter, and playfulness.

Overall, I want you to recognize that balance is important. Banter and flirting is fun and exciting, and most women, especially the great ones, will engage in it. However, you must balance the banter with substance or you will never get what you want from a woman.

The essential piece to any interaction with a woman is connection.

Connection is needed in every situation with a woman. One-night stands, dating, long-term relationships, marriage, and every other possible situation require connection. Without connection, you will never truly have a woman. Even though banter built on pick-up lines and routines can be fun, you had better have something else to offer or else you will go home alone.

Angry, Bitter Men Do Not Get Laid

Never in the history of the world was a bitter, angry, frustrated man laid. Unless he paid for it, but I guarantee whomever he paid was not happy about it. Every day I get hundreds of emails from great men. Every day I also receive emails from men who are frustrated, which can turn into anger and then bitterness. It is so hard for me to get through to them, but trust me I try. Sometimes it works and sometimes it feels like I'm banging my head against a wall!

Overall, I realize that many men are frustrated due to their negative experiences with women. I get that. I know many women who are in exactly the same place. Because of their experiences, they put up walls and make it difficult for any man to get close to them. I would tell the same things to these women that I am going to say to you: as long as you keep these walls up and maintain the belief that all members of the opposite sex are evil, you will never get what you want. Those walls make it impossible to make a real connection with anyone else!

I want to share a great email I received from a guy who, with my help, finally let go of his frustrations and suddenly saw results with women.

Marni,

You won't remember me but about a year and a half ago, I hit one of your blogs. I stupidly left a rant of all my anger and frustrations towards women. You responded back to me with a really warm but firm response. This made me take a hard look back at my life and I realized women were not at fault. I was for pushing them away when they tried to get close.

After this introspection, I began to change my life by working out three nights a week with my cousin and joining the local art association photography group. There are some real pros there and they are impressed with my work. I'm 43 and now have twenty something's hitting on me. I need to clear two final hurdles.

Excise my limiting belief women do not want to be with me and being able to ask these women out. I have missed a few opportunities last year due to this one. I am working on these. I accept responsibility for my lack of a girlfriend and am working towards this goal. I apologize for the length of this missive but wanted you to know you helped.

Thank you.

Loved this email!

Believe it or not, emotional blocks or false beliefs about women can actually hurt your chances with women. They may not be as major as this gentleman's were, but they can still have a huge effect on you. My husband used to have a huge mental block, not towards dating, but marriage. He used to think that marriage was the first step to divorce. Awesome for his romantic interests, right? In his mind, if he and I were to get married, then it would ruin our relationship and we would divorce. However, his ultimate goal was to have a family. He was torn. He had to work hard to change the story he had been telling himself from "Marriage equals divorce" to "Marriage is about commitment and love. Marni and I will work hard to keep our marriage strong. I want a family and we can make this work."

Minor tweaks in the stories we tell ourselves can totally alter the way we move forward in the world. I call this "re-framing" and it has been popping up a lot lately with the guys that I work with. Many have horrible stories that they tell themselves every day. For example:

- "I'm horrible with women."
- "I have no idea how to talk to women."
- "I am a bad lover."
- "Women will never want me."
- "Women are evil."
- "I am bad at relationships."

I firmly believe that if you do not talk nicely about yourself, no one else will. I gave each of these men an assignment to reframe what they say to themselves aloud for a whole week. So instead of saying "I can't approach women in public," say: "I feel nervous about approaching a woman in public, but I know that I want it so I am going to do it. It will not be as bad as I have imagined."

No Woman Likes a Pouncer

Just like the rest of my generation, I fell in love with Tigger from *Winnie the Pooh*. Remember that adorable, pouncy tiger? It was not until recently that I realized Tigger was a horrible influence on the youth of today. He preached about pouncing and how it was fun, fun, fun, fun, fun! Pouncing is not and should not be fun because it can get you into trouble!

In my business as a Wing Girl, I encounter men who impulsively respond to their emotions and pounce on women. Pouncing usually occurs when a man meets a woman he is attracted to and wants her to feel the same. He wants to be perceived as the perfect man. He calls constantly, shares feelings too quickly, is overly available, and compliments for no reason. You get the picture.

Unbeknownst to men, these actions scream out that they are needy, dependent, and desperate. All attributes that women are very turned off by. Why is it that this behavior is unattractive? One would think that attention and the showering of emotions would be flattering to a woman. Not so. This type of behavior turns them off faster than you can say ketchup!

Why is this behavior so repulsive to women?

It is repulsive because it is not manly. It is weak behavior from a male who does not understand his own value. He sacrifices his self-worth for the attention of an attractive stranger. As a woman, I find it strange when a man who does not know me is willing to drop everything in his life to please me. He knows nothing about me. Why is he so eager? I automatically assume there is something wrong with him. I then proceed to dodge his calls, make dates through text message that I will eventually cancel at the last minute and try hard to avoid seeing him ever again.

Many of my girlfriends who find themselves in similar situations respond exactly the same way. It is too much, too fast. Many of the men who I work with used to act this way towards women. They would pounce and then be completely crushed when a woman did not respond favorably to their romantic behavior. I would enlighten these men by telling them what their behavior was saying to women and get them to admit to why they were acting that way. Most of the men admitted that this type of behavior stemmed from insecurity, discomfort, and confusion. Once we get those emotions in check and work on building self-respect and confidence, we usually find that the pouncing stops and they start to see better results with women.

My clients learn that the more they value themselves, the more women feel the same way about them. There is no need to pounce. Instead, they take their time and evaluate whether or not they want to invest further in a woman. They finally understand that they are involved in the choice to connect. So single men of the world, listen up. Be strong, respect yourself, and leave the pouncing to Tigger! Remember, there's a reason that he's single.

Do Money, Social Status, and Possessions Matter To Women?
Email:

I always feel insecure if I meet a girl who has accomplished more than I have or has a better job.

So, am I right or not?

Jordan

My response:

Jordan,

Well that insecurity, my friend, is what is going to turn off a woman--not how much you have. Just because a woman is more successful than you are or has more than you does not mean that you are less of a man. What you have does not matter to most great women (Don't bother with gold diggers, shallow women, etc.) What matters is when you let it affect you and make you self-conscious about it.

Women are not bothered until you voice that you are bothered by your money, social status, or possessions. If you are a negative, freeloading bum who complains about where he is in life but does not change the situation, then women will not find you attractive, at least not in the long term.

However, if you are positive about who you are, your job and what you have, then she will be too. As long as you always remain true to who you are and strive for greatness, she will be happy. If not, then you have to evaluate the person you are with.

Women want to know that they have a partner who is proactive about making a great life with her. That does not mean yachts and partying at clubs. It means character, support, and love. For those who you feel are more accomplished remember that you also have areas that you are accomplished in that she may not be. Never feel below another person. Learn to respect and acknowledge what you and others have achieved.

Marni

Why Do Women Respond to Me When I Act Like an Asshole?
Email:

I am a passive, easygoing person. Girls never really showed much interest in me. Then, just as an experiment, I tried acting like an asshole and many girls liked me more. There was more connection. Why do girls like it when I act like an asshole?

My response:

The thing is that you are actually a nice guy, so your version of acting like an asshole is actually just you acting like a guy with an edge. Deep down you are not an asshole and women can tell that right away. Women love playfulness, challenge, and teasing. They do not like when a guy bends over backwards for them without even knowing them and gives up all his self-worth.

You have tapped into something amazing. You have gone from passive to active! It is super sexy and you are getting results.

Marni

Do I Need To Be Funny To Get The Girl?
Email:

I purchased your video and audio program from your website. First, I have to say it was amazing to be able to hear how all those women really talk when men are not around. It was great and I got a lot from it. I did have one question on something said. In the video with you and your friends, someone says that she wants to be approached in a fun way, with some funny comment.

Now, I understand that but there is not always something funny to comment about. Is it okay to just go and say, "Hi? What's your name?" Sometimes women say that they want men to be direct but also subtle, confident but not cocky, etc. It's confusing, you know!

Adam

My response:

Adam,

I totally understand how you could find that comment confusing and frustrating. It is not always easy to bring the funny, especially when you are not naturally an over the top funny guy. What she was saying is that she wants a man who does not take things so seriously all the time and can see the humor in things. Bring something to the table other than your deep understanding of how to write the best HTML code man has ever seen.

This does not mean you have to perform, be the entertainer, or work hard at making her feel good. It means you have to bring something to the table to add to her evening. I have had many men who approach me and bring nothing to the table. No character, no energy, just a bag of nerves, no confidence and expect me to make all conversation. For me it feels like pulling teeth. It takes away from my night.

I am a nice girl and will give at least five minutes of my time to a man that has the confidence to approach. I am patient. Most women will not give you that time and if they do, it will be followed by a lot of head nodding, one-word answers, and the hopes of finding an excuse to get away from you.

I go out to have fun. I work all day and when I go out, I want to enjoy my evening not do more work. So bring the fun, enjoy life, and be able to laugh at yourself. That is what women mean when they say sense of humor is super important.

Marni

Is It Wrong To Date Women You Know You Do Not Want?
Email:

Marni,

Is it wrong to date women knowing that you have no romantic interest in them at all but are doing it to gain experience? Someone I know advised me to do this. I find it a little bit misleading to do this. Very similar to women receiving attention from men knowing they have no interest in being romantic with that person. Maybe my thinking is wrong, what do you think?

James

My response:

Hmm, that is a sticky one.

I would not ask a woman out that you are not at all interested in just so you can practice dating. However, if you are on a date and you realize, "Eh...I'm not really into this girl," that is okay. Then you handle it like a man and tell her you are not really feeling it.

I get what your friend was trying to advise. He wants you to get out there, practice, and not be so fussy during this time. I would say be looser with who you deem datable but I would not date girls knowing you are using them.

Seems like that could bring bad karma and I am not even into karma. My rule of thumb if you ever have doubt about your actions is to think to yourself, "Would I want someone to do that to me?" If the answer is no, then do not do it.

Marni

How Long Should I Keep Up The Game?
Marni,

I am attempting to learn the judicious application of mystery. I have been playing with it to some success. I actually enjoy it. I can indulge the novelist in myself. My question, how long should I keep up the game?

Andy

Andy,

Games are meant to be played when you are younger or on vacation, not all the time. You can be mysterious, but when you decide you like a woman, that is when you start to share. You can still hold onto your information. Meaning be private and do not throw it all on her at once.

There is no need to continue to be completely mysterious otherwise, she will get bored and move on. Worse, she will become insecure and angry and you do not want to see that. Trust me.

Marni

2. Surprise! The Things They Do Want.

The Short, Bald Man That Turned Me On

To illustrate just how unimportant certain stereotypes of attraction are to women, I want to tell you a story about a night I spent out with my girl-friends. It wasn't a particularly special night but we were going to make the most of it - a hip bar in Los Angeles with my amazingly hot girlfriends.

When we first got there, we scoured the bar to see if there were any potential hot men. We spotted a group of guys and plopped ourselves down next to them, making sure they could see us. As we sat down, they looked over at us, smiled, and then huddled together, glancing our way between bouts of conversation.

Then one guy turned to our table and asked "What are you ladies drinking? My friends and I want to buy you drinks." Of course, we said yes! After the drinks arrived, two of the guys came over to our table and started gabbing on and on about a huge financial deal they had just closed. One of them then talked about a new car he had just purchased, and he did not forget to mention the price.

I looked at each of my friends and could see each was individually giving the "help me" eyes. The help me eyes are an international female signal that say to other women, "Help me. I want to get away from this guy." It is very subtle and difficult for men to see if they are not aware of the practice.

To see an example of the help me eyes go to:

http://www.winggirlmethod.com/get-insider-her-bonus

I waited until we had finished our drinks, so as not to be rude, and told the guys we were meeting friends and wanted to go find them. As soon as we moved, the topic of conversation shifted immediately to how ridiculously those men had acted. We could not believe that attractive, well-dressed men, who were obviously successful, were that insecure!

Why did they feel the need to babble on about what they had when they could have just talked to us? Trust me; at least half of us would have gone home with one of those men. However, they totally ruined it and turned each of us off.

About two hours later, I was getting drinks from the bar when a man approached me. He was about 5'6", was wearing glasses and I could see myself in his head from five feet away. Not attractive but for some reason when he walked over to me I felt the energy that I can only explain as magnetic.

Here's how the whole thing went down:

He came up to me and said, "Hi my name is xxx," and held out his hand. I introduced myself.

X: "You're not from here are you?"

To access FREE bonus materials go to:
http://winggirldatingtips.com/gih-bonuses/

Me:"No. How can you tell?"

X: "Because you are the only girl in the bar smiling and looking people straight in the eye. Girls like that do not exist around here. Where are you from?"

Me: "Toronto in Canada"

X: "I just visited Toronto. Great city, it's like a much cleaner version of New York. What made you want to move here?"

The conversation went on for some time and that excited feeling in my stomach kept increasing. He was interesting, confident and had this comfortable way about him that intrigued me greatly. When I like a guy I am talking to, I get nervous, trip over my words and ramble. Sometimes about topics that have absolutely nothing to do with the conversation at hand. Lucky for me, guys seem to like that.

I did not notice anyone else around me. I was totally into this guy.

I took a second to think about it. What is it about this bald, short man in glasses who has absolutely no style whatsoever? Then I realized what it was that I was attracted to, his character. This guy was interesting and confident and obviously, a man who went after what he wanted. He was light-hearted, did not take things too seriously, and did not agree with everything I said.

He looked me straight in the eye and went after me, without a doubt in his mind that he might be rejected. He did not approach me with some cheesy line or routine. He approached me directly without fear and I could sense that. He did not dominate the conversation. If anything, I was doing most of the talking. This in turn made me nervous. I was the one who was afraid of possible rejection.

I did not feel at any time that I had full control of the situation. I re-member thinking, "Does this guy like me?" "Am I sounding smart enough?" "Is there lipstick on my teeth?" "My mouth hurts from smiling." In a short period, he made me feel comfortable, excited, and special. I could tell from our conversation that xxx was a good man and desired by others. This of course made me want him more.

He was self-assured, calm, and cool and collected. This is the type of man that creates attraction. The type of man I want to date and be in a relationship with. As long as you are direct, confident, and clear in your wants, women will be attracted to you. The more comfortable you are in your skin, the more attractive you are to women.

I am attracted to a self-assured man who knows himself and knows what he wants. This attitude makes me feel special and lucky to have captured this man's attention and makes me want to see him again. I can tell you that xxx was not always able to approach women with such confidence. Later, he revealed to me that he used to be unsuccessful with women and was afraid to approach. He used to think he was too skinny, short, and unattractive and it took time to grow into his looks.

After years of working on himself, he feels comfortable in his own skin and can approach anyone without fear. You too can feel exactly like xxx. Every man can! You can approach, attract, date, and keep the most attractive, amazing women.

Do You Have The Presence Women Want?

I am always talking about the "presence" of some men that makes women fall head over heels. A while back, I received an email from one of my clients who wanted me to elaborate on just what the heck "presence" was and why he did not yet have it. Below is the email from X. He really got me to dig deep and I know this information is the exact information you need to understand what women want from a man.

Question from X:

Hey Marni,

If looks do not matter that much to women, what is the point, or the deed, or the key or whatever, to get the woman to stop looking at what he looks like, and start to like him for who is inside?

More so, what must the man be like, act like or do in order to take attention away from the way he looks and turn a woman's attention to his character?

What would make you forget about how the guy looks and like him for something inside?

X

Answer from me:

I am going to try to break it down for you the best way that I can. For me, yes, looks are what initially catch my eye. They are the first and only thing I can use to evaluate whether I am interested. However, looks are quickly overpowered as soon as I start to feel a man's character. This can happen in a matter of seconds or it may take minutes.

I wanted to share a little story with you that may be able to help explain what I mean when I talk about presence. The other day, I was with a best guy friend of mine who has always been great with women. Some of our other friends are a little jealous of his abilities and credit it to his money, car, or home.

As a woman, I know that his success with women has nothing to do with his status. Honestly, he could be dirt poor and bald and women would still be super attracted to him. In fact, they were back when he had nothing. The reason why women are attracted to him is his calm demeanor, confidence, and enjoyment of life. He is easy to be around, interesting and has his own point of view but is intrigued by what others have to say.

My friend knows he is awesome. Not in an arrogant way, but in a humble way. I know what you were looking for was a more magical answer than this but that is really the secret. Now the hard part is getting to a place of believing this about yourself and feeling that same calmness and comfort.

I may not be able to give you a magic pill that will get you that instantly but I can tell you how to get it. This type of character is built from practice, experience, and information. It comes from observing, people but more importantly from recognizing yourself. I do not want to sound like a spiritual guru right now but I hope you see where I am going with this.

My guy friend has been in therapy since he was 12. He was constantly evaluating himself with the assistance of another person. This allowed him to face his greatest fears, learn to control his anxiety and come out on the other side as a man of value. The reason he has this value for himself is that he has worked at it and earned it. He gives himself permission to go after what he wants and believes that he will get it. If he doesn't, then that is okay too. There will always be other opportunities.

You can have this presence if you want it!

Marni

When a man approaches me, I of course evaluate him on his looks. As I said before, I have nothing else to go by. Then something interesting happens. As I get a better sense of his character, his face starts to morph. Sometimes it can get better looking and sometimes it can become hideous.

As happened with X when he approached me with surety and confidence despite his appearance, my attraction grows based solely on someone's character and personality. I hope what you took away from this email exchange with X is that the only person holding you back from getting everything you want is you. The more you push yourself to take chances the more confidence you will gain and more opportunities with women will appear.

You Must Turn Yourself on Before You Can Turn a Woman On

This man gets what turns a woman on! As a woman, I felt attraction for him just reading what he wrote. That's how powerful it is.

Email from M:

Dear Marni,

I want to thank you for all of your wonderful advice. I have been subscribed to your newsletter for the past couple of months and can definitely say that I have seen an improvement in my interactions with women. I think that the female perspective you provide does wonders that no other male PUA's can imitate. I think I really understand what you are trying to get us guys to realize that we have to like ourselves before a woman can. Guys have to approach every situation knowing they are worth it and if a girl rejects them, then she is just missing out on being with a great guy. I like to think of it as follows: I am a great guy who is in a boat going down a river. On the riverbanks, there are tons of women and every now and then, I stop and offer one of them the chance to get on board the boat with me. If they do, great! If they do not, then there is just another girl further down the river that will get on board and have a great time with me.

I find that since I adopted this mindset, girls have looked at me differently, giving me more attention, and allowing me to enjoy flirting more. It's as if they need to get on board that boat with me or else some other girl will take their place.

Thank you for allowing me to realize this, Marni.

M

Again, this honestly turned me on just reading it. To feel like this in your gut, you have to get out there. You have to push yourself, take risks, interact with women, be rejected, and laugh, gain experience. It all starts with one-step, so get off your butt and start interacting with women.

Why Confidence Is More Attractive Than a Six-Pack and Cash
When I created my program, "How to Become a Man Women Want," I polled hundreds of women and asked them

To access FREE bonus materials go to:
http://winggirldatingtips.com/gih-bonuses/

what they found most attractive. Do you know what 95% of them said?

Confidence.

Looks are way down on the list. Why is confidence so attractive to women? What is it about a confident man that turns us on so much? I will tell you.

1   A confident man does not need a woman; he wants a woman. Men who are needy are very unattractive and women can instantly feel it when a man is needy.

2   A confident man is proud of who he is and understands his value. If you do not think you are good enough how will she think you are?

3   A confident man is comfortable at all times. When you interact with a woman and you get uncomfortable you stop yourself from connecting with her. How can a woman be into you if she does not feel a connection?

4   A confident man makes a woman feel safe and secure.

5   A confident man is a masculine man. If you approach a woman without confidence, expecting her to step into the dominant male role and lead the approach, she will feel more masculine than you will, and all attraction will be lost. Women want to feel feminine not masculine. The more feminine you allow a woman to feel the more attracted to you she will be.

There are a million more reasons why confidence is the most attractive characteristic to women. So as a man, how can you build this confidence? How do you even start? Lucky for you I have the answer to both questions here.

I picked up a famous women's magazine called *Glamour*. It's a great way for me to keep in touch with recent female trends, wants, and desires. There was a great article in the issue called, "Your Get-Confident Kick Start" written by Vicki Norton (Norton, 2012). The article teaches readers how to build confidence. Even though this article was targeted at women, Vicki's lessons apply to men as well.

In fact, a lot of the advice is quite similar to the advice I give my private coaching clients. I want to share the highlights with you. Each of these little tips are easy to absorb and a bit more challenging to apply, but if you do I guarantee that within three months' time you will have the confidence every woman is attracted to.

"People who ooze confidence are prepared to take a risk and do their best. It's okay to acknowledge that you don't feel confident all the time, but if you decide to do all the things you want to do anyway, your confidence will grow."

-DR. CECILIA D'FELICE

"Remember people who appear to be 100% confident are often over compensating for insecurities and putting up a protective facade. To gain some ground, put yourself out there and into situations where you might initially feel out of your comfort zone-then you'll realize you can change.

-DR. ANNA SYMONDS

"We know your lack of confidence is all your mother/ father/ brother/ teacher/ boss/ ex's fault but get over it. By blaming them for your inadequacies, you allow other people to control your destiny. To move forward and be the person you want to

*be, the first lesson is that shyness and low self-esteem are
optional, not fixed."*

-DR. JAMES

Practice, practice, practice! According to Dr. Russ
Harris there are five factors leading to low self-confidence:
harsh self-judgment, excessive expectations, preoccupation
with fear and anxiety, lack of skills, inadequate experience.
Practicing your skills (picking up, talking to, or approaching
women) and gaining experience are essential.

Feel the fear.

*"The golden rule for developing genuine confidence is this: the
actions of confidence come first, the feelings come later."*

-DR. HARRIS

Snap out of it.

*"Realize that everyone is so busy worrying about
themselves, they're just not that interested in how you're
coming across."*

-DR. SYMONDS

*"Take it step by step. Set goals and split them
up into manageable stages."*

-DR. D'FELICE

Confidence is not a magic formula that you can
stumble upon in a book or on the Internet. You must work to
attain it but when you do, it will give you everything you need
to walk up to a woman and be yourself.

Four Things You Need To Do To Get Women

At the beginning of every New Year, I sent out a reminder message to everyone that follows my blog and reads my newsletters. It is my virtual Kick in the Ass motivator. Every year I want to change it but every year I realize that what men need to get women does not change all that often. It is a permanent thing.

I want to share that annual letter here because it is just as poignant now as it would be in January:

1   **Be a Leader, Not a Follower**. I know it is easier to be the "laid back guy" but it is certainly not attractive. Be decisive in everything that you do. Even if you do not have an opinion, form one and take it to action. For example, "X, what do you want to do tonight?" Your typical answer: "Doesn't matter to me, whatever you like." New answer: "Let's go to this new Whiskey bar I heard about."

2   **Get a Life**. Women are more attracted to men that have lives of their own. Why? Because it means they are not as needy.

3   **State Your Intentions**. It is time for honesty - No more covering up your intentions and suppressing your masculine urges. If you see a woman you find attractive, go get her and let her know what you want. Moreover, what do you want? You want to know whether she is a good fit for you. Whether it has to date, have sex, form a partnership, build a friendship or whatever. You will never find out unless you are clear with your intentions.

To access FREE bonus materials go to:
http://winggirldatingtips.com/gih-bonuses/

4   **Be Direct**. There is nothing sexier than a man who is direct. Be direct and ask for what you want. Think of how you asked for gifts from Santa when you were younger. You asked for what you wanted "I want a BB gun, I want a Nintendo, and I want a G.I. Joe." Then it was up to Santa to say yes or no. The only way to get what you want is by asking for it. I guarantee that if you start doing these four things, you will get what you want with women!

Three Things Women Find Sexy That Have Nothing to Do With Sex

Believe it or not, some of the sexiest things you can do to turn a woman on happen outside the bedroom. Below is an email from one of my clients. Together we have taken him from a pouncing pleaser to an attractive option to women. He sent me an email today listing the discoveries he has made over the last year. He now lives by what he shares here:

Email:

Hey Marni,

I should preface this by saying that I am not perfect. I still make mistakes, sometimes screw up, and end in the Friend Zone. However, these are my discoveries...

1   Passion for Life. You have to be living a life that you feel passion-ate about. At some point she is going to want to know about you, and you are in good shape there if you have some cool stories of your own to share with her.

Doing aerial and Cross fit and learning to surf was terrific as far as helping me meet women, not so much due to meeting women at these places, but more because it gave me something great to talk about when I did go on dates.

A statement that always seems to turn on women, "I really want to try (worthwhile goal), and so I have been (preparing for worthwhile goal)."

2   Self-Control. This takes on a bunch of different forms but here are a few that mean the most to me. You cannot be in any rush to share these stories. Let her talk, and then you can share. You will not only look courteous, but it is also smart. The less you talk, the less likely you will end up sticking your foot in your mouth! If she never does ask you about your life, then that is a good sign that she is not someone you want to get involved with.

- *You have to be comfortable with carrying your end of the conversation and let her carry her end. This means that you cannot be so quick to fill in the silences. Let there be pauses.*

- *You have to learn how not to become fazed if she tells you something that is impressive or intimidating such as, "I played professional beach volleyball and now I model," or, "I run my own business and have so much money I never have to work again."*

- *Genuine appreciation is hot. However, be very careful about giving too many compliments! The irony is that the more of them you give past the first one, the less genuine they actually look.*

On the one hand, we want to make the girl feel comfortable, but on the other hand, we want the girl to invest in the

To access FREE bonus materials go to:
http://winggirldatingtips.com/gih-bonuses/

interaction too, and worry just a little bit how she is coming across.

3   Self-awareness . The ability to check in, see how you are feeling, and see what is really going on. I'm feeling unsettled because the conversation does not seem to be going anywhere good. When I asked her a perfectly nice question about her job, she just seems to be complaining. "Okay, it's her problem. Let's see what we can do to turn this around." Or, "I'm feeling nervous right now, and so I feel an urge to talk. I'm going to hold my tongue for a couple of seconds at least and see what happens."

I know there are more. These are mine for now!

Mike

These three things are essential, not only for women, but also for you as a man. It took a while for Mike to grasp these concepts, but now that he has, the world of women is his for the taking!

Real Men Take Risks
"For hundreds of thousands of years of human development, a confident attitude was much easier for men to gain and display than it is now because it was required for survival. There was hardly any choice. Until recently, the demands of physical survival were the primary issue in pair bonding and confidence-building roles for both sexes directly related to survival were far more apparent. I am not talking about survival in extraordinary circumstances, either. It could be as basic as steadfastness in getting the crops in out of the rain."

—DANA PEACH

What I read from this is that confidence was much easier to gain in the past. Men were constantly faced with potential risk; risk of not eating, risk of being attacked, risk of disease. The list goes on. Every day, there was a large or small risk that every man faced to survive. Today's man faces no risks or challenges, unless they are self-imposed. He can be safe, comfortable, and sheltered from harm's way if he so chooses. Sadly, many men make this choice.

My challenge to you is to incorporate a small risk into your life every day. Here a few to get you started:

1   Smile at five strangers today.

2   Approach any woman you find attractive, say "Hi." Then leave if you want. The risk is merely the approach.

3   Ask out the woman you have been putting off asking out.

For the next five days, take these risks. If you have a hard time remembering to take these risks, put them in your calendar or write them down on a Post-It and place it on your computer screen. Whatever you need to do to remember to take these risks, do it. If you do not, you cannot grow. If you do not grow, you will not gain more confidence. If you do not gain more confidence, you can never become a man that women want.

I challenge you to take these small risks every day. I promise that if you do, you will become a man women want. More importantly, you will gain more confidence and the character you have wanted for a long time.

To access FREE bonus materials go to:
http://winggirldatingtips.com/gih-bonuses/

Rules for Attracting Beautiful Women

I have an exercise for you. It requires minimum effort and will create maximum results. Ready? I want you to know what it is like to walk in a woman's shoes. No, I am not going to make you put on a pair of heels but I am going to show you what beautiful women experience with men every day.

You are going to see it all from a woman's point of view. I hope that this exercise will give you a new perspective on what women deal with on a daily basis and how you can change to get what you want. So that you can see the tiny errors and mistakes you make that are silently killing your chances of attracting, dating, and getting incredibly amazing and beautiful women, here is your assignment.

Your assignment is to create an online dating profile as a woman. Pick a dating site, make your profile, and post a couple pictures of a sexy woman (find some on the Internet; trust me, there's plenty.) Now wait for the responses that you get.

One of my clients wrote to me after doing the exercise:

Email:

Marni,

I signed up on a dating site as a woman and I have learned that dudes are lame. In less than a day, I have received 11 pages of e-mails, most of which have "Hi" as the subject. The message itself is usually something along the lines of, "You're pretty, please talk to me." I used some photos that I found online (lots of interesting sites pop up when you Google "hot babe").

In a few of the messages, the guys were not so subtly bragging about one thing or another. Alternatively, they just hit me with a barrage of questions. I didn't realize how pathetic most guys are. Is this what it is like for women in real life to? I am almost starting to feel like I would be doing women a favor by approaching them.

Dave

My response:

Dave,

There it is! The magic realization. Yes! You would be doing them a favor to save them from the horrible shit they are bombarded with every day.

Yes, women get that in real life.

Yes, the more attractive a woman is the more bullshit is thrown at her and the lower quality level of man approaches her.

I am so glad that you stand to see it through a woman's eyes.

Marni

Here's another response I got:

Hey Marni,

I just wanted to say that this exercise is genius!

At first, a part of me felt somewhat bad for fucking with all those desperate guys after posting a pic of an insanely beautiful girl, but another part of me just wanted to laugh my ass off at all the redundant, mundane messages I got.

To access FREE bonus materials go to:
http://winggirldatingtips.com/gih-bonuses/

In the very first day, that I had the profile on, I got 17 messages. 15 out of 17 had either, "Hi," "Hey," or, "Hello" as the subject line. Are you kidding me? That is the best they can come up with?

I thought that was bad until I read the actual messages. Pretty much all of them said something to the tune of this, "Hey. You are beautiful.

Message me back and get to know me." A woman would probably pick up from this email several things.

- *The guy has no creativity.*

- *The guy is very shallow. If the first thing he mentions is your looks that is obviously all he really cares about.*

- *He is probably very desperate as the email is so simple and boring that he probably sends the same exact email to multiple women every day. I have to admit, I was once guilty of this myself.*

Thanks again for the exercise. It definitely opened my eyes. By the way, I took the profile down.

Alex

I have given this exercise to over 200 men and each of them have had the same response. They were shocked at how women were bombarded by pathetic losers. You can imagine why women have developed their own "barriers for entry" and why it is even more challenging for great men to break through the barriers. Try it. Learn from it. Change your perspective because of it. Something tells me I am about to get in a lot of trouble from dating sites but it is worth it.

Women Want a Strong Man

I debated the placement of this email exchange for a few days. In fact, I probably moved it around from chapter to chapter over a dozen times. The reason I did this was that the email below is from a man asking to get his girlfriend back. This comes way after understanding the type of man women want.

However, at its core, the question is really about the type of man women want and how this guy can become that man. Therefore, I stuck it at the end of the first chapter because I feel it truly explains what all women want.

The honest to God truth about what women want is everything and nothing all at the same time. We do not know what we want. We may think we do, but usually we are wrong. After almost a decade of working with men to explain the ultimate mystery that is women, I have realized what women truly want, even if they do not know they do.

What women truly want is a man. A man that can lead us towards what we want from life. Not by being an aggressive, arrogant jerk but by remaining strong, confident, and comfortable no matter what we throw their way. A man, who gets us, understands us, leads us, and can stay grounded in our moments of confusion. That is a man any woman would happily be attached to, and feel satisfied that she is getting everything she ever wanted from and more.

Now that we got that out of the way, I want to share an email exchange with a guy whose girlfriend broke up with him for not being a man. Seeing as he has a penis, I can understand his confusion with her statement.

To access FREE bonus materials go to:
http://winggirldatingtips.com/gih-bonuses/

Above, I told you what women want and now, through my email correspondence with C, I am going to show you what exactly that looks like.

Here's how to be the strong man women want.

Email:

Marni,

My girlfriend and I just broke up two weeks ago. Well, she broke up with me mainly for not being a man. Not in bed (our sex was always amazing, and I know it was for her to), but for not being a man in the other areas of my life. The short version of the story is that I had been lazy, without a job collecting unemployment and not taking my own life seriously. I ended up being evicted, and had to stay with her for the last two months and even though I had already started to get my shit together, the damage was already done, and my actions were not fast enough for her, and I totally agree. I got the boot.

Now I always told her that if she really loved me at my lowest point in my life, she was really going to be crazy about me at my best. I have always been fairly successful at having my shit together (before I met her), but for the last three years I went somewhere (mentally) I swear I will never go back to. I didn't even recognize myself. So, she waited, waited, and watched as I moved towards my goals at a very slow speed. For a year and a half, this went on. I am surprised she lasted that long with me. I know I would not have put up with it if I were in her shoes.

Having said that, my life is finally turning around. I have my own place, I am starting a new job next week, and my new business is finally generating some revenue. Now that I purchased your programs, I know I'm on my way to become the man every woman wants and I want to start using this knowledge on her because I know that once she sees the new me she's going to feel different towards me.

I want a second chance not so much at the relationship, but at us. I want her to see the real me plus all this knowledge and to date her nonexclusively and see where it goes from there. I know we still love each other very much but I was acting a bit needy and clingy towards the end, which I know, turned her off.

When she broke up with me, she told me that the only time she felt a connection was when we were having sex. After reading some of your material, I can see that crystal clear now. We had been talking (before we broke up) about how we could not wait to watch the Roast of Charlie Sheen, which is this coming Monday. We have not spoken to each other for a week now.

I wanted to text her tomorrow or the next day, invite her over, and cook crab legs since that is our favorite meal. I have a feeling she will say yes (at least for the sex), if I play it right. I was going to text her: "Hey, the Roast of Charlie Sheen is Monday. Why don't I pick you up and we will watch it at my place? Thinking of having some Cajun & garlic crab legs for dinner. "

I don't know what to do. Should I even bother? I do want her to see me for the man I once was and the new man I am becoming. Thank you very much! You are the shit for helping men like me in this area.

Carlos

My response:

Carlos,

Thank you for being so honest with me. I have a good picture of what has happened with your ex and I have a few suggestions on how to move forward.

I think there is some emotional work that needs to be done here before inviting her over for the roast. From what I can tell, she is waiting to hear that things have changed, that your outlook has altered and that you love yourself almost as much as she did. For a woman, feeling that you have invested poorly can be one of the most damaging and heart wrenching things to experience.

I would love for you to talk to her about everything that you are working on. The things you are doing to better your life and better yourself. I know you may think either she knows these things or that you have told her. I want you to let her know definitely that you understand she broke up with you because you were not being a strong man. It took her leaving for you to see it and now that you do, you are working on creating a truly great self.

Here is my advice: email or invite her over for the roast, and when the night is almost over, tell her. However, you must remember to stay positive, strong and most importantly, I want you to convey that you are doing this for yourself, but that she inspired it.

If you leave all of this unspoken, it will take a lot longer to get back together. If you are honest, positive and show you have confidence, the "getting back together" process will be a lot quicker. Overall - this girl wants to see that you will not go back to that dark place. In that dark place she loved you, but was not attracted to you. That is not a good place for a relationship.

Marni

His response:

Hello Marni,

Thank you very much for your quick response. It helped me out tremendously. I invited her over to watch the roast and she gladly accepted. Instead of me telling her what I wanted to say, I wrote her a letter and gave it to her towards the end of the night. Not very manly, but I wanted to make sure I didn't forget anything and I knew we were going to be drinking wine and if I had waited to tell her when the night was almost over, I probably would have gotten a bit too emotional, maybe forgotten something and she probably would have been too drunk to remember. She put it away, spent the night here with me, and didn't read it until today.

(I included a copy of the letter in this email. Any input you could give me on how different I should have said anything would be greatly appreciated so I can learn from my mistakes).

The whole night was a lot of fun filled with lots of great sex, laughs, food, and some hot tub action. More importantly, I was acting like a total man this time really listening to what she was saying, looking at her in the eyes and I used the word "because" many times when I was telling her a story. I also took my time before I went for the first hugs and kisses of the night and when I did, she was all over me with sparks in her eyes. Before, I used to be always all over her right away so I know she saw a few things that were different about me.

So I went to her place later on today to drop off a makeup purse and a shirt she left here (her car is not working that's why I went there instead of her picking them up herself). When I was there, she gave me a hug and kissed me. I sensed something and I asked her if she was okay to which she said:

Her: "Your letter blew me away!"

Me: "Why?"

Her: "That was exactly what I've wanted to hear, not for me, but for you."

Me: "Yeah"

Her: "You know I love you, right?"

Me: "I know. You know I love you too, right?"

Her: "Yeah"

We kissed and hugged like the old days. I got up to leave and we walked out together because she was leaving too. There again we kissed again like old days. It was very passionate. Later on she text me, "Thanks for everything. I had an awesome time." I replied 30 minutes later with, "You're welcome. I enjoyed it too." Normally I would have responded right away with a more enthusiastic response but I wanted to continue the new tone and not go over the top.

Doing that felt good. We have been texting back and forth for the last several hours talking about her work mostly. I have been taking my time responding, giving her a lot shorter responses than I used to and basically letting her do 75% of the talking but still leading the conversation. I feel very good about how this is going, but I have to continue taking good care of myself and not put her before me (which is hard for me). I am not going to do that ever again.

Thank you very much. You are a genius!

Carlos

I can say this a million times in a million different ways but men are always going to roll their eyes at me. Here goes. Women do not care if you are rich or super attractive or have abs of steel. At the core, we really do not care about any of that. Those are bonuses. What we want is a man who is grounded, comfortable in his own skin and can be strong.

I have added Carlos' email so that you can see how perfectly he expressed himself. He expressed his emotions to his ex without becoming emotional. Only a strong man can truly do this.

Email from Carlos:

Listen, there's something I want to tell you. Don't worry, it's all good.

I know the real reason you broke up with me was not because I didn't have a job, but rather because I wasn't being a strong man. I completely understand that now. The fact that I didn't have a job had something to do with it yes, but that wasn't the main reason. And I know that. And looking back now, I can totally see that crystal clear. I totally see now how on top of all that stupid behavior, I had also been acting needy and clingy and no woman wants that. But the truth is, I didn't realize I was doing that. I knew I was being lazy. I knew I was fucking up, but other than when we were having sex, I had no clue I wasn't being a real man with you. And I know you told me, but that was during a fight. At that point I took it as an insult and not as constructive criticism.

And on top of all that, it really sucks that we both had to see that really dark side of me that day when I was drunk and called you names and I was considering suicide the day before. I have never been in that place before and I made a promise to myself that I will never go back there ever again. In fact, none of this is going to happen to me ever again. That much I am certain of. I can tell you, when I lost my mom I was hurt. But nothing like that Tuesday Aug 30th, 2011 when I almost totally lost it. That was by far the worst day of my life. And for the record, I wasn't contemplating suicide because my girlfriend broke up with me. The main reason was because I was totally broke, no job, no gas in my car and basically homeless. Not that that makes any better, but that was the reason behind those crazy thoughts. I have always been very positive about life even in the darkest of times but for the first time in my life, I felt totally hopeless. And I hope you can forget that day because I have already forgiven myself for it and put it behind me. And I'm not going to apologize anymore either because I have already done that enough times to last us a lifetime. I don't need to feel sorry for myself anymore. That time has come and gone.

I want you to know that because of this whole experience, I have already changed. But I also know I still have a lot of work to do. And I'm not saying this to try to get you back either. I am well aware that I don't need to be in a relationship anytime soon and when I do, I'm going to be with a woman who wants to be with me as much as I want to be with her. I am saying this because I want you to know that I am not changing for you, I am changing for me, but you were the one who inspired me to do it. It took an event such as you leaving me so I could see how fucked up I was. And I want to truly thank you for it because now I find myself standing on solid ground on my own two feet with a crystal clear picture of the man I want to become and the man I will become. I want to be a man every woman wants to have and I already know I'm on my way there because I can feel it. I am in a much better place now that I'm looking ahead. Now it's all about me. It's about me getting my self respect back, my self worth back and become not only the man I once was, but a much better man. Like I said before, a man every woman wants to have. That is my number one priority right now. Nothing or no one else matters at this point.

I want you to know that I think you're fucking amazing. I really do think so. It's the truth. You really are. And I know I didn't say it enough before but I think that if I had said it, it would have made matters worse being that I was already acting like a total pussy being all needy and clingy. But now, I can honestly say it without any fear because I have nothing to gain from it, or lose. You are an amazing woman and any man would be lucky to have you. Don't ever change, especially for someone else. I am very proud to have called you my girlfriend for the last 1 ½ year and I had a blast with you. I really did. So once again, thank you so very much for inspiring me to become a better man. You have no idea how thankful I am, and I will always be...for the rest of my life! That much I know for sure.

Love,
Carlos

Why Women Like 50 Shades of Grey

I just finished reading 50 Shades of Grey and my libido is pumping! I totally get what all the fuss is about. If you haven't seen a woman reading 50 Shades of Grey yet, where have you been? Women are flicking through this thing over lunch, browsing it on the subway, and reading it aloud at their book clubs. They are wildly turned on by this simple piece of fiction.

50 Shades of Grey explores women's sexual fantasies. It is a book about sex, erotica literature, and it has the entire female population mesmerized. I highly suggest you get yourself a copy as it is a direct insight into the female libido!

Before you rush to the store to pick up a copy, I wanted to share my thoughts on it with you. Because I feel this is one book, where you need a woman's opinion to guide you through the hidden details in it as to what women find so attractive, as it may not be what you think!

I do not want you to read this book with your masculine goggles on. I want you to see it from a woman's point of view. Because once you do, you will have unlocked the secret to every woman's hidden fantasies, and be able to seduce any woman you want.

Here's the bad news: not all women want to be chained up, spanked, or blindfolded. Do not think, "Oh that's what I have to do, string a woman up in ropes and use her as my sex slave because that's obviously what all women secretly want." Remember, the book is fiction, and the relationship is exaggerated.

However, while you may not be a 27-year-old billionaire with a helicopter there are a few valuable lessons you can learn about what women want that I want you to notice. Many guys reading this book will assume that the reason Ana Steele is so interested in Christian Grey is that he is young, good looking, and rich.

Nevertheless, the female readers cannot actually see Christian Grey; they cannot take a ride in his helicopter. What really engages them, what really turns them on, all occurs

To access FREE bonus materials go to:
http://winggirldatingtips.com/gih-bonuses/

within the mind. There is not actually any sex until way beyond 100 pages in!

What does that tell you?

That sexual tension, for women, is in the mental anticipation of what might happen. It is her not knowing if she can control herself, and how he is going to seduce her. It is not about jumping right into the whips and the chains: it is about Ana feeling like Christian really wants her, and building up her expectations. Christian frequently says things like, "If I want to I will..." He is leading his own life and vision, and women love that! Now you can use something similar: try telling a woman that you want her to check out a restaurant or a band you think she will love. This is so much better than speaking in a weaker, less certain way.

Being direct is not the only thing that makes Christian Grey attractive though: he also makes Ana trust him; he shows her that beneath his suave exterior there is vulnerability. He mentions past traumas and at times, the mask slips, he is not as perfectly in control as he initially makes out. Rather than being a turn-off, this makes him more attractive to Ana. She feels like he is sincere, he is passionate and that there is something deeper happening, that he is in love with only her.

He shows that his entire attention is on her and frequently tells, "You are mine." In the book, this can come across as possessive behavior, which is not attractive. However, I want you to take from experience that women like to feel desired by men that a man is not just with her because he has no other options, but because he truly wants to be with her.

So when you are reading <u>50 Shades of Grey</u> remember that it is an erotic fantasy and to read between the lines. Women do not want you to be a billionaire, but they do like a man who has authority and confidence. Women do not necessarily want a man to dominate them, but they do want a guy to adopt the masculine role and lead. Women do not want a guy who owns them, but they want to feel desired and wanted.

Do you know what the best lesson you can take from 50 Shades of Grey is? That women love sex too, that they want to meet men, and that this book has woken up the libido of thousands and thousands of women all around the world!

II. How to Approach and Meet Women

"I can tell when guys are checking me out. When I catch them, they look away

when what they should do is smile at me"

—WING GIRL HEATHER

More than 50% of the earth's population is female, and virtually all of them are available to you, (within a reasonable and legal age range.) This is not ancient Rome, pre-partition India, or the Monarchy. When it comes to dating, society is more liberal than it has ever been. There is no caste system, there are more interracial marriages today than ever before, gay marriage is legal, and we can find love at any age, in any place. What does this tell you?

- You have more options than ever before.

- You have the freedom to choose someone you really want.

- You have all the time in the world to do it in.

In this chapter, I will tell you where to find the one you want, how to approach her, and how to deal with rejection. Yes, there will be lots of it. Women are everywhere. This should be fun.

1.   The Where and How:

Where to Meet Women

Think there are no women in your town, your state, your country? You are single because there just are not any women, right? I don't think so. One of the most common hurdles guys tell me that they face is that they don't know where to find women! I want to give you an insight into how to overcome this so that you know that not meeting women is really due to your mindset and not the reality of the situation.

You may not live on Broadway, NYC, or South Beach, MIA, or Hollywood, CA, but here are my top places to meet women in your local area:

1   **The Mall:** Without making any jokes about how much women like to shop; one of the key places to meet women is where they hang out during the day. If you are attracted to someone, it is perfectly ok to strike up a conversation while you are going about your day-to-day activities. So next time you see a cute woman shopping for some groceries, buying a coffee, or window shopping, approach, approach, approach. Unless you go and say, "Hi," you will never know!

2   **The Gym**: You are killing two birds with one stone
here; getting fit and meeting women! I know you
may think that women do not want to be
bothered at the gym, and this is somewhat true,
but it is a great place to slowly build rapport with
women and make connections. Over the years, I
have dated seven guys that I met at the gym. One
was my trainer but the others were guys who just
went to the same gym as me.

3   **Social Clubs**: Once women have left college (and
gained some responsibilities) grinding at a dance
club until 3am loses some of its appeal! However,
there are plenty of other social opportunities. If
you live in a city, check out networking events;
often these list attendees, including single women.
If you live a little further out, then look into local
social clubs, book clubs, yoga clubs, etc.

4   **Explore Your Hobbies**: Have you always wanted to
learn a few skills in the kitchen? Try out rock
climbing, or finally make the trip to see your
favorite band play? Then do it! Not only will you
build up your own social life (which instantly
makes you more of an interesting guy to be
around) but you will also end up meeting women
who have a shared interest with you: great for
kick-starting conversations!

5   **Get Online:** Even if there wasn't a woman for
hundreds of miles around, the fact that you are
reading this means you have access to the
Internet. So get online, try out a few free sites, put

some effort into getting a good profile together, and whip out those icebreaker messages. Just like in real life, Internet dating requires you to be pro-active, but it can be a great way to meet tons of people you might otherwise never run into in real life.

6   **Ask Your Friends**: Most people still meet people through their social circle, so it is time to work on yours. A group of good friends will get you off your couch and out meeting people. The bigger your social circle is, the more people you can meet who are a friend of a friend of a friend. So start saying 'yes' when people invite you out, arrange cool social gatherings and tell all your friends to play matchmaker!

7   **The Grocery Store**: I think I have officially increased revenues at Whole Foods and other local supermarkets around the world, because I tell every guy I work with to go practice meeting women at the grocery store. It works so well and it is a great place to meet women. In addition, it has many conversation starters because there is much to observe: "You have a lot of sweet potatoes" or "I've never had that type of fish before, what does it taste like?" Plenty of ways to break into conversations.

8   **Google!** Google is the best resource for finding events, groups, and activities you can participate in so that you can meet women. I actually use it for most of my one-on-one clients.

Here's how to use it:

- Enter your age or age range you are looking to meet/interact with.

- Enter singles events/singles groups/singles parties.

- Enter your city (see example below.)

A whole bunch of options will pop up. Then go through the options and find the best choices for you. Make sure to do one of these things each week and I guarantee you will meet women or new single friends that you can hang out with. No more being the third wheel! You now have a list of eight ways to find places to meet women! So no more excuses, it is time to get off your butt and make it happen!

How to Meet Women While Travelling
Marni,

Give me a little advice. I have a hard time meeting women as my job is on the road. This means I am traveling all the time and living in hotels. My question is about how to meet women while traveling alone.

Jason, 34, Chicago

My response:

Google   los angeles, single events, 30's

Jason,

Traveling for work can be a bitch on your social life. It requires extra effort and possibly some risk taking on your part. If you are up for it, and I hope you are, I have five steps on how to meet women while traveling alone below:

> Step 1: Before going to any city, do your research. Choose the best hotel location for going out and being social. You do not want to be stuck out in the boonies if you plan to be social and meet women while traveling for work.

Tip: Most cities have websites set up to tell you what is going on socially for restaurants, hotels, nightlife etc. Find one of these sites and select three things you would want to do while in that city.

> Step 2: Go to the lobby or hotel bar and scout for others flying solo, male, or female, doesn't matter. You are just looking for a partner to go out with at this point. Tell them you guys are going to go out for a fun night and give them 1 or all of the options you had selected. Trust me, if people are at a hotel by themselves, eight out of 10 times they will be up for some sort of interaction and social outing.

> Step 3: Go to the social location.

> Note: If you are not into clubs, do not go to clubs. If you are, go. I usually suggest a local bar. They are typically busy and filled with people who are up for new experiences.

Step 4: Start interacting with others. If you have a hard time doing this you can introduce some sort of game between you and your new friend. For example, guess her name. It's a game where you both guess which half of the alphabet the first letter of her name falls. If you are right, you get a beer and vice versa. This game is meant to get you in a fun mood and gives you a reason to approach. When you approach with a reason, you will appear more confident and more attractive to women. Plus, it makes the approach a hell of a lot easier.

Step 5: Start pulling others into your game. You are up for a fun night so make it memorable. Be a leader and gain the attraction of others in the bar. If you follow these five steps on how to meet women while traveling alone, I guarantee your business trips will no longer feel so depressing and lonely. Whether or not you meet a woman, you will enjoy your night.

Marni

When Should A Guy Approach A Woman?
Email:

Marni,

Late last night, I went grocery shopping. Upon going to checkout, I saw a woman that I was extremely attracted to.

While we checked out, I decided to take a different path to my car only to find out that she was parked near me. She was wearing biking gear and had a bike in the back of her truck. I think this intimidated me a little because I did not approach her. Reason being, I really thought I would be bothering her. I do this all the time and want to stop wasting great opportunities.

My question to you is, "When can I approach a woman?"

Ian

My response:

Ian,

The short answer to your question is always. If you see a woman you want, approach her. Remember, it's about you first, her second. It sounds like there is a lot of pressure on your approaches and you may be thinking large picture instead of small picture.

Large Picture: I am going to approach this girl, she is going to be attracted to me, I am going to get her number, we are going to date, and have sex.

Small Picture: That girl is cute, I want to talk to her and see if I like her.

Having the small picture in mind before any approaches will make it a lot easier on you. If you do not attach a large picture outcome to your actions, then you may not feel as much pressure to succeed. I want to comment on one other thing you said in your email where you said you thought you would be bothering her. I hear these assumptions from the men I work with all the time.

Assumptions gone wrong:

"She's not my type"

"She won't be into me"

"I'm too short for her"

"I'm too fat/bald/skinny for her"

"She probably has a boyfriend"

"She's busy right now"

"She doesn't want to be bothered'

"She's with her friends and doesn't want to be interrupted"

It's very interesting that these men know so much about a woman they have never spoken to before! What I find more interesting is that so many men are mind readers. These assumptions are fears disguised as intelligent justifications. These are what I like to call 'conceived truths' that stop us from getting what we want. Please do not fall victim.

Approach every woman that peaks your interest and decide what category you want to put her in after you have some facts to base it on.

Marni

Get Off Your Ass and Start Practicing!

You want to know the secret to picking up women? Get off your ass and approach them.

You are never going to meet a woman if you:

To access FREE bonus materials go to:
http://winggirldatingtips.com/gih-bonuses/

- Sit at home and moan about how you can't meet women.
- Don't approach the women you want.

So how do the successful guys do it? How do they know what to say? When to touch her? How to make her want them?

The guys who are successful did not start as natural superstars. Well some of them did, but the majority of the men who are great with women learned their skills through practice. They got off their butts and approached. They were rejected and were turned down repeatedly and over again, until they built up their confidence and started seeing results.

Where am I going with this? I have been fascinated with routine and self-discipline lately (mainly because I didn't have either.) So what did I do? I scheduled, created a system, and am now training myself to become more disciplined in my day-to-day work life. It is challenging and exhausting but it is paying off. I am seeing results. It is the same thing for you in your quest to figure out how to pick up women. It all starts with pushing yourself and figuring out what works best for you.

Does Practice Really Get Results?
Email:

Hey Marni,

I definitely fall into that category of guys who read a lot but do not practice enough. If I want to change that, I guess I am back to going out and doing approaches again. Which I admit I am not crazy about just because I do have so much trouble with it. However, what I figure I will do is start with just saying something, anything, and not worry about what happens after that. I guess just try and do this every day.

Thanks Marni,

Dave

My response:

Dave,

First, no more sad talk. I can hear how discouraged you are through your writing. A little tip is that if you start using more uplifting words and expressing yourself more positively you will actually become more positive.

A little chicken before the egg science shit. Now on to your question. It's not about approaches. It's about understanding that giving yourself one month of going out once or twice a week is not going to get you the results you want.

If you wanted a job, you would not put out three resumes and hope you get a bite. You would go to a recruiter (online dating), reach out to your contacts (friends and friends social gatherings); you would research companies who are hiring and contact them (cold approaches). If you have done all these things many times over then you are doing enough. If not, you still have many fun times ahead of you!

Right now is your research phase where you can screw up, take chances, and experiment without fear. Because it is all for you. So get out there, start approaching, and see what works for you.

Marni

Is She Testing Me?
Email:

Hi Marni,

I had an experience today in which the outcome surprised me a little bit. I went to the hairdresser's at a new place that I had not been before. I was talking to the girl who was cutting my hair and we were getting along quite well, good conversation etc. It was nearing the end of the day and the other girls working there went home, as it was quiet.

At this time, she did not worry about keeping her voice down as much and actually introduced herself to me, without me even asking her name (which I thought was a good indication) but in the next few moments she proceeded to tell me that she has a husband, which took me totally by surprise! Why would she bother introducing names?

I was going to ask her out, but I am a nice guy so not after I heard that. Was it just a trap or a test?

Cheers,

Justin.   (I just downloaded your course this week, learning a lot so far!)

My reply:

Justin

Whoa! Whoa! Whoa! Slow your roll. Trap? Test? Not at all. Just because a woman is in a relationship does not mean she has to remove herself from social society. Women, even women in relationships, are certainly allowed to engage in harmless conversation with a man they have no intention of dating.

Think about it this way: You confidently started talking to her; she talked back, was engaged in the conversation, liked the conversation, and was having a good time talking to you. Is that a bad thing? No. Did she lead you on? No. In fact, she did the opposite.

To ensure there would not be any confusion as to what "this" was, she let you know she was in a relationship. This is her silently saying, "I don't want to give you the wrong idea and lead you on? I am enjoying talking to you."

Honestly, she may not even be thinking that at all. She may just be thinking, "I'm in a good conversation with another human being." Done! Women are not out to get you and they certainly are not out to test you or put you through the ringer. This woman was just engaging in conversation with an obviously good conversationalist!

Marni

How Do I Handle Female Cock Blocks?
Email:

I was out the other night talking to this girl and within two minutes of talking her friends came over to see what was going on. Then, after another two minutes, they pulled her away. Why are women so nosy?

Neil

My response:

Neil,

Women can be nosy for several reasons:

1   Jealousy: They are bitter and want some attention too.

2   Protectiveness: Until that woman knows you, who you are and why you are talking to her friend, she is not going to trust you. Men rape, men break friends' hearts, and men may have hurt her in the past. She sees herself as loving and the protector of her friend.

3   Disapproval: Since she does not know you she has nothing to base her disapproval for you on other than past experience. Her ex may have looked like you so in her mind she knows the kind of guy you are by your look.

4   Unaware: Some women are just so caught up in their own shit that they really are not even aware of others.

5   Caring: The girl you were talking to may have just had a bad breakup so her friend thinks it's best for her to stay single, have fun and enjoy herself. This is linked to protectiveness.

So now, you have five reasons as to why women are "nosy." However, the most important thing to recognize is that the girl did not come back to you again. Her friends do not have that much power over her to keep her away from a guy she may or may not like.

Tip: One thing you could have done was befriend the whole group instead of "keeping" the woman away from her friends. Another is asking for her number if she came back to you.

Marni

How Do I Build Attraction and Take It to the Next Level?
Email:

Dear Marni,

I'm 28 years old and currently live in Minot, ND.

The most important thing about women I want to understand is on how to build attraction and take interactions to the next level. I can go up to women and have conversations, but I usually see myself being put into the "Friend Zone."

What I really want to know and understand is how to shape my interactions so I put off an attractive, sexual vibe. In addition, I want to know how to take things to the next level, from conversations to getting into a relationship and getting physical.

Thanks, Richard

My response:

Richard,

This is a great question and a very common one. As a woman, I have tons of guys approach me. I am not a fool and I usually know what they want from me but they always pretend they want something else. Meaning they act friendly as not to set off my "he's attracted to me" alerts.

The truth is I would rather he set off those alerts and be straight about his intentions. That's what I am attracted to, and that is what I want to be with. Please know, I am not saying to be an aggressive, abrasive jerk. I am advising you to know what you want and ask for it.

For example, you see a girl you like so you approach her and start a conversation. The "what you want" portion should be, "That girl's cute, she caught my attention, let's see if I like her more."

Falling into the Friend Zone happens for so many guys because at first, to not set off her "hitting on me alerts" or "he's attracted to me" alerts, they approach as friends. The intention for these guys is "she's cute, I don't' want her to know I want her, cause it will freak her out, and then I want to get her number."

First, it creates too much pressure for you. Second, it feels fake and dishonest to her. Third, it creates a big wall stopping any type of connection between the two of you.

My advice: Be clear with what you want from women and then ask for it. State your intentions; do not hide them.

Tip*: In the first 30 seconds, touch her on one of her three trigger spots: lower back, forearm, or upper arm for no longer than one to two seconds. I would say to do these one or two times in a three-minute conversation. This lets a woman know you are not approaching for friendship.*

Tip*: Remember that you respect yourself more than you respect her. At least I hope you do since you have only known this woman for 30 seconds. That means, know what you want, see if* *she is what you want and if she is what you want, ask for it in a clear manner. It's all about you, until you decide it is about "us."*

Let me know how that goes,

Marni

2.   Body Language and Headspace

How to Show Confident Body Language When Approaching Women

Body language is an important topic so I write about it frequently on my blog. One of my most popular posts in recent years was how to show confident body language with women. One of my previous clients, Alastair, wrote in, commented on the article, and let me know that he has been doing some extensive research in the field of body language.

Here's what he wrote:

"The body language stuff has always interested me alongside behavioral psychology. I've been studying both subjects for the last two years and I have to say that I love being able to utilize the skills in my communication with women."

Ready for some specifics?

Nine Tips for Confident Body Language

What would you say is the most important factor when approaching a woman for the first time? If you think it's all about delivering a killer opening line, then think again. When approaching a woman, it is not about what you say but how you say it - it is not about the verbal, but the non-verbal. It is often said that when meeting someone for the first time, the other person forms up to 90% of their opinion about us in the first 90 seconds. That's an important first minute and a half!

Furthermore, research suggests that body language forms between 60% and 70% of the meaning we digest from verbal and non-verbal communication (Hazell, 2011) with tonality of voice being in second place, and the words we actually say being third. Some influential experts, such as James Borg, even go as far as to suggest that body language makes up 93% of human communication. That leaves a very small chunk of the communication for the words that come out of our mouths.

We have established its importance; let's now have a closer look at some examples of confident body language. In the following pages you will find nine body language tips that you should consider incorporating into your approach when approaching a woman. To become truly natural and competent with these ideas, they should not be part of an act. Do not pretend to be someone you are not. Instead, reshape your understanding of how to connect and communicate with others.

- **Have Confidence in Your Approach**. Do not be timid or tentative. A man who is self-assured and assertive will approach in a casual manner, without hesitancy or uncertainty, as if walking over to greet a friend. Stand up straight to make the maximum out of your height (you can lose inches by slouching). Keep your head up, revealing the throat area a little (a good sign of confidence) and push your shoulders back (pushing your chest out a little). This is a good, confident posture.

To access FREE bonus materials go to:
http://winggirldatingtips.com/gih-bonuses/

- **Approach from an Angle if You Can**. Do not approach from behind and try not to approach from directly in front as it can seem aggressive, which may make the lady feel uneasy and put her on the defensive.

- **Be Warm and Friendly**. Look into her eyes and smile. I cannot over-emphasize the importance of the smile as you approach - it shows you are not posing a danger and that you are open and fun. You can take this further - a wry, cheeky smile will add an element of mystery to the mix. Be passionate and enthusiastic - you are having a fantastic time and you want to share the experience with her. Remember my Golden Rule : you will impress if you express.

- **Keep Your Hands in View**. People naturally feel less comfortable and trusting when other people approach them with their hands hidden and it can be a sign of dishonesty. So, be as open with your posture and your hands as you can.

- **Take Up Space**. Confident, alpha-males take up space and their arms flow naturally and freely when walking and gesturing. If you approach looking hunched up and tense then it will come across that you are not confident in who you are, which is a big turn-off.

- **Relax**. Once you have approached and started talking to her, try to relax as much as you can (this naturally comes with experience) and do not put pressure on yourself. The less you are worried about the outcome of the conversation, the more you will find yourself relaxing and the easier the conversation will flow. If you are on edge, it will put her on edge. Try not to fiddle and twitch - fiddling with your watch, cuff links (think Prince Charles), jacket, or other objects is a pacifying gesture and demonstrates nervousness, as does taking excessive sips of your drink. If you are a naturally nervous person, this is definitely an area you should work on.

- **Stand to the Side**. When talking to her, do not stand directly in front of her. Instead, stand either at an angle or at side-by-side. The advantage of standing side-by-side is that you can use your surroundings as part of your conversation. If you have a drink in your hand, try not to hold it between the two of you as this forms a barrier.

- **Engage the Group**. If you are approaching a group, make sure you engage the entire group - do not just focus on the woman you most like.

- **Mirroring.** I have deliberately left this one until last. It is an idea that comes from the NLP (Neuro-Linguistic Programming) world and involves the mimicking of voice tonality and body language to create rapport. The important thing to emphasize with this is that, if you are going to use it, it needs to be subtle. In life, we naturally mirror the body language of people we have rapport with. By being aware of this, you can use the mirroring technique (mimicking some of the elements of their non-verbal) to accentuate the rapport between the two of you. You can consider mirroring breathing rate, body posture, gestures, facial expressions, and speech patterns. Be aware - if you get this wrong and you are not subtle with it, the woman will sense it and it will creep her out.

That's nine tips for confident body language. I will just take a moment to re-iterate my comment from earlier. With these ideas, consider integrating them into your everyday life rather than using them as an act when you approach a woman. By doing this, you will be far more successful and you may begin to notice that other elements of your life improve at the same time, your work and business life, for example.

Consider practicing these ideas with everyone you meet. That way, when you see a woman you are attracted to, your approach will flow naturally.

Remember that change is all about breaking habits, so you may feel uncomfortable implementing these ideas at first. Just try them out one by one and see what works for you. Do not be afraid of going wrong when you are practicing - that is how we learn. Get practicing and start looking forward to being a more confident you.

A Smile Is an Inexpensive Way to Change Your Looks

The first step to being attractive to women is very simple: you need to smile more! I came across a disturbing article that read, "A note to single dudes: If you're looking to pick up a woman at a bar, whatever you do — don't smile at her." This is based on a new University of British Columbia study (Tracey, 2011), published online to the journal Emotion.

Their findings said that women are actually less sexually attracted to smiley, happy men.

Before anybody starts taking this study and the directions posted in the article by Melissa Dahl too seriously, I wanted to add my thoughts. First - this study is correct. Women do not like men who smile. However, not in way that you are thinking. When I see a man out with his friends, enjoying life, relaxed in his own world and smiling, I think, "He's sexy. I totally want to get to know him."

However, when I am with a man, I just met and he is beaming from ear to ear with a big smile on his face I think, "He's nervous, he's fake, this is making me uncomfortable, and why is he so smiley, he's super needy, he must be on something, and I want to go home."

You have to remember that women are scanners and evaluate people on many different levels. This evaluation is subconscious. It is not done out of bitchiness. It is a form of protection against inconsistent and harmful men. For women, a smiling man is attractive, as long as he has a valid reason to smile. If there is no apparent reason, a red flag goes up, followed by an emotional reaction that leads to distrust and a drop In attractlon.

This study was conducted on women's responses to pictures of men (not moving images). This provided similar results as the OkCupid study that said profile pictures of men looking off camera were more attractive to women (Rudder, 2010). This provided very similar results as the OkCupid study that said profile pictures of men looking off camera were more attractive to women?

To access FREE bonus materials go to:
http://winggirldatingtips.com/gih-bonuses/

A man in a picture, who is looking away from camera, is interesting.

What is he looking at? Who is he looking at? Moreover, why is he not focused on me? That is what women are thinking. That is why both the University and OkCupid drew similar results from their studies.

Do not let these study results stop you from smiling. Women love a man that smiles! It is a certain type of smile that totally gets us every time. I love when guys smirk at me. I find it so sexy and mysterious. It says to me, "I'm awesome, and have my shit together" but in a non-arrogant way. Think Robert Pattinson or George Clooney. Flashing a smile when you see a cute woman walking past lets her know that you are interested in getting to know her better. It also says, "I'm confident and I've got things to smile about." A smile is the universal signal for 'I'm a happy, positive person, come say 'hello!' Get into the habit of smiling. Smile at beautiful women in the mall, an art class, the gym, work, a coffee shop, or a bar, and start engaging them in conversations.

It sounds easy but smiling is not an automatic reflex for everyone. Like other skills, we can train ourselves to do it. For example, when I was interested in what people were saying to me, I used to furrow my brow.

I didn't realize I did this and that my furrowed brow sent a message to people that I was judging them, or communicated to them that I did not like them. Therefore, I worked on it and made a conscious effort to not furrow my brow. I couldn't remember, right off the bat, not to furrow my brow. It had been a habit of mine for years. I used a little trick to remind me to soften my brow and keep smiling!

Back when I wanted to get over my approach anxiety, I used to wear a rubber band around my wrist that I would snap to remind me not to be afraid and to get back into my body. Once my approach anxiety was gone, I used the rubber band on my wrist as a reminder to ease up that brow and smile. It took a few weeks of me snapping my wristband to remember what to do, but soon my frown pretty much vanished.

I soon noticed that people seemed more relaxed around me, and responded more warmly. This is because I was signaling that I was approachable, and that I was appreciating what they were saying. Smiles are great communicators, and do a lot of the hard work of approaching a woman for you. If you have trouble remembering to smile, or have a natural 'frown face' when you meet new people; you need to develop your own technique to encourage smiling.

If you have a serious expression, (even when inwardly you feel happy) then you may need to find your own version of my reminder-wristband. Maybe try another special accessory or item, or every time you become conscious that you did not smile take ten seconds and plaster a smile across your face, so you get into the habit of beaming.

Here are a couple of things you can do to become more comfortable with smiling. Use a real smile that does not seem forced or fake and those women will not view it as insincere and unattractive.

Is the Initial Smile Essential?
Email:

Hey Marni,

I am 22 and have been doing a lot of work on myself to be better with women. Anyway, on to my question. When I see a woman I think is attractive anywhere, I have problems just simply smiling. For example, I would look at her and she would look back, but the last thing on my mind is to smile at her. People always tell me to smile more, but my normal face simply does not have a smile on it. I have a sense of humor and am always cracking jokes with my friends, but it takes time for me to let go with strangers.

Also, it is important to note that I usually do not randomly smile, as I am usually thinking of something else and partially zoned out. I mean, I am aware of my surroundings, but I am usually trying to figure something out in my head.

Is this initial smile essential?

Julian

My response:

Hey Julian,

I want to be honest with you. You are way ahead of the game. Most of the men I work with come to me when they are in their mid-thirties. Honestly, you are ten steps ahead and it's awesome you already understand and own the "who the hell cares" mentality!

In regards to the smile, I used to have something similar. When was interested, I would furrow my brow. I did not realize that my furrowed brow sent a message to people that I was judging them or that said to them I didn't like them. I worked on it and made a conscious effort to not furrow my brow.

At first, it took me wearing elastic around my wrist to remind me to not furrow my brow. I would look at the bracelet and that would trigger me to not furrow. Eventually, I could trigger myself because I would notice when I was doing it and I would immediately soften my brow. Now I still do it, but not as often as I did before.

Overall, I noticed that as soon as I stopped furrowing my brow at people I was talking to and softened my face; they would immediately relax and seem to like me more. I was more approachable and they felt that I was appreciating what they were saying, which made them feel good.

Great outcome from a little work!

Marni

25 Famous Thinkers and Their Inspiring Daily Rituals

Many find it interesting to glimpse inside the lives of famous thinkers in an effort to understand where such creative thought and intelligence is rooted. In that vein, here is a peek into the routines and rituals that writers, philosophers, and political leaders have depended on to keep their work on track and their thoughts flowing. Explore the daily rituals you may want to incorporate into your life.

1   **C.S. Lewis**. Writer and thinker CS Lewis had a very clear schedule of his day, with activities such as work, walking, meals, tea, and socializing down to the very hour they should be done. He even describes

when beer should be enjoyed (not at 11:00 for fear of running over the allotted 10 minutes for the break.)

2		**John Cheever**. American writer John Cheever wore his only suit of clothing each morning as he rode the elevator down to a basement room where he worked. Upon arriving there, he would undress to his underwear, hang up his suit, and get to work. He would dress to go back upstairs for lunch and again at the end of his day when he would ride the elevator back home.

3		**Fred Rogers**. Do not doubt that Fred Rogers was indeed a great thinker, despite the fact that he is best known as the familiar Mr. Rogers from the long-lasting PBS children's show. His television show was a safe place for many young children, by his design, and he fought hard, in his quiet manner, for the show to stay on the air. The famous routine that started and ended his show was not the only routine in his life. Each day he would wake at 5:30 and begin his day with reading, writing, study, and prayer. He would take a swim most days of his life, take a late-afternoon nap, and go to bed at 9:30 each night. Perhaps the most idiosyncratic of his rituals was that he kept his weight at 143 pounds his entire adult life. He saw his weight one day and realized it aligned with the number of letters in "I love you" and vowed to maintain that weight, which he did.

4		**Stephen King**. This famed writer keeps to a strict routine each day, starting the morning with a cup of tea or water and his vitamins. King sits down to work between 8:00 and 8:30 in the same seat with his papers arranged on his desk in the same way. He claims that starting with such consistency provides a signal to his mind in preparation for his work.

5 **Gertrude Stein**. This famous writer discovered inspiration in her car. Apparently, she would sit in her parked car and write poetry on scraps of paper.

6 **Immanuel Kant**. Kant would begin his day with one or two cups of weak tea and a pipe of tobacco. While smoking, he would meditate. He would then prepare for his lectures; conduct lectures from 7:00 to 11:00, write, then have lunch. Lunch would be followed by a walk and time with his friend. The evening would consist of a bit more light work and reading.

7 **Barack Obama.** Taking care of physical fitness and family are two important elements of President Obama's daily ritual. He starts his day with a workout at 6:45, reads several newspapers, has breakfast with his family, and then starts his workday just before 9:00 in the morning. He may work as late as 10:00 some evenings, but always stops to have dinner with his family each day.

8 **Alexander Dumas**. Whether or not he had heard the adage about keeping the doctor away, Dumas, the author of The Count of Monte Cristo and The Three Musketeers, started each day eating an apple under the Arc de Triomphe.

9 **Benjamin Franklin**. Franklin kept to a tight schedule, starting his day waking at 4:00 am. Until

To access FREE bonus materials go to:
http://winggirldatingtips.com/gih-bonuses/

8:00, he would wake, wash, eat breakfast, and think about what he would accomplish for the day. From 8:00 to 12:00, he worked. Lunch was from 12:00-1:00, where he ate, read, or looked over his accounts. He then worked until 5:00. The evening was filled with dinner, cleaning up, music or conversation, a look back over his day, and then bed at 10:00.

10   **Haruki Murakami**. This popular Japanese novelist sticks to a specific daily schedule that begins at 4:00 when he awakes. He writes for five or six hours, and then either runs 10 kilometers or swims 1500 meters (sometimes, both). After his workout, he reads and listens to music until he goes to bed at 9:00. Murakami claims that writing a novel requires both the physical and mental strength that his routine provides.

11   **Franz Kafka**. Kafka started his day at his job at the Workers' Accident Insurance Institute from 8:30 to 2:30. Afterward he would lunch until 3:30, then sleep until 7:30. Upon waking, he would do exercises and have dinner with his family. He began writing at 11:00 in the evening, usually working until 1:00 or 2:00 in the morning-sometimes later.

12   **Toni Morrison**. Writer Toni Morrison describes not only her daily routine, but also the importance of rituals to writers. Morrison describes her own ritual involving making a cup of coffee and watching the light come into the day. Her habit of rising early was first formed as the mother to three children, but after her children left home, she discovered a routine of her own, that still includes early mornings. Morrison urges all writers to look at

what time of day they are most productive and what type of surrounding is most conducive to their work to help form rituals that will promote creativity.

13   **Ingmar Bergman**. This famous director, writer, and producer of film and drama demanded quiet and set schedules. While working on a play in 1996, he was reported to stand outside the rehearsal hall half an hour before rehearsal to ensure the actors were not socializing. He had a set time for beginning work, taking lunch, and ending work. He disliked noise, meeting new people, and crowds of people. While he aspired to a quiet life of writing without deadlines on the island of Faro, he could not actually stay with his retirement, and returned to the scheduled life of work. He was still working just a few years prior to his death in 2007.

14   **Charles Darwin**. In his middle and later years, Darwin stuck to a very rigid schedule that started at 7:00 in the morning with a short walk, then breakfast. He would then work throughout the morning. Lunch, at 12:45, was his biggest meal of the day. His afternoon was also scheduled and consisted of two walks, reading, and backgammon. Darwin could not tolerate much socializing, and kept it to a maximum of 30 minutes at a time.

15   **Kingsley Amis**. This British comic novelist and poet were also famous for his love of alcohol. He kept to a strict routine of writing in the morning until about 1:00, when he would take care of his dressing and shaving, then begin the afternoon with a drink and a

smoke. He would work until lunch at 2:00 or 2:15, sometimes going back after lunch to work and sometimes not. He considered any work accomplished in the afternoon a bonus. When the bar opened at 6:00, he would fortify himself with more alcohol and work again until 8:30.

16   **Winston Churchill**. While Churchill's routine may not be for everyone, it seemed to revolve around lots of food and drink. He would rise at 7:30 and stay in bed until 11:00 where he would eat breakfast, read several newspapers, and dictate to his secretaries. When he finally got out of bed, he would bathe, take a walk out-side, and then settle in to work with a weak whisky and soda. Lunch began at 1:00 and lasted until 3:30, after which he would work or play cards or backgammon with his wife. At 5:00, he napped for an hour and a half, then bathed again and got ready for dinner. Dinner was considered the highlight of his day, with much socializing, drinking, and smoking that sometimes went past midnight. After his guests left, he would then work for an-other hour or so before heading to bed.

17   **Aldous Huxley**. This famous thinker and writer would start early each day sharing a breakfast with his wife. He would work uninterrupted until lunchtime. After lunch, he and his wife would go for a drive or a walk, and then he would return to work from 5:00 to 7:00, and then have dinner. After dinner, his wife would read to him until almost midnight. Due to an eye illness early in life that left Huxley with very poor eyesight, he relied heavily on his wife to do many activities for him besides reading. She often typed his

manuscripts and was even reported to have cut his steak for him at dinner.

18   **James Thurber**. Another writer with difficulties seeing, Thurber would often compose his work in his head at almost any place he found himself. His wife would recognize the look in his eyes and interrupt him mid-paragraph while they were socializing at a party, and his daughter saw him retreat into his private world over dinner. His method later in life was to spend all morning composing his text in his head, then between 2:00 and 5:00 he would dictate about 2,000 words to his secretary.

19   **Gunter Grass**. This German writer starts his day at 9:00 or 10:00 with a long breakfast that includes reading and music. Afterwards, he begins working, taking only a break for coffee in the afternoon, and finishes at 7:00 in the evening. He claims that he needs day-light to work effectively. When he writes at night, the work comes easily, but upon reading it in the morning, appears to be of lesser quality.

20   **John Grisham**. When Grisham first began writing, he still had his day job as a lawyer. In order to do both, he stuck to a ritual of waking at 5:00 and showering, then he'd head off to his office, just five minutes from home. He had to be sitting at his desk with a cup of coffee and a yellow legal pad by 5:30. He gave himself a goal of writing one page per day. Sometimes this page went as quickly as ten minutes while other days required one or two hours. After

finishing his daily page of writing, Grisham would then turn his attention to his day job.

21   **Gerhard Richter**. Famous German artist, Gerhard Richter, sticks to the same basic routine he has for years. He wakes at 6:15 and makes breakfast for his family, then takes his daughter to school. By 8:00, he is in his studio, where he stays until lunch at 1:00. After lunch, he returns to this studio until the evening. He claims that his days are not usually filled with painting, but with the planning of his pieces. He puts off the actual painting until he has created a kind of crisis for himself, and then pours himself into it.

22   **Simone de Beauvoir**. French writer and lifelong companion to Jean-Paul Sartre, Simone de Beauvoir reported that she got bored if she did not work, and tried to work every day except the few months she would take off to travel. While writing, she woke with tea, and then began her work around 10:00. She would work until 1:00, then have lunch and socialize with friends. At 5:00, she would resume working, usually at Sartre's apartment, until she would stop for the day at 9:00.

23   **Jean-Paul Sartre**. In a letter Sartre wrote to de Beauvoir some thirty years before her recounting of her daily working routine, Sartre describes his days, which are noticeably similar to the pattern later described by de Beauvoir. Sartre writes about waking early and having coffee in a cafe, then reading, teaching classes, and private lessons, then lunch. After lunch, he would do more reading and letter writing.

24   **Jacques Barzun**. This French-born American historian and cultural critic celebrated his 100th birthday just two years ago and still enjoy a life of routine and work. He starts his day at 6:00 with coffee and the local newspaper, followed by 45 minutes of exercise, then a morning of work in his study. He spends his afternoon reading. Cocktails are at 6:30, followed by a light dinner. Barzun's evening is spent reading the New York Times, no TV, and bed by 9:30.

25   **Ernest Hemingway**. Hemingway described his writing ritual as starting just as the sun began rising, then working straight through until whatever he had to say was said. He likens completing his morning of writing to making love to someone you love, being both empty and fulfilled at the same time. Upon completing that morning's work, he would wait until the next morning to begin again, going over his ideas in his head and holding on to the anticipation of starting again the next day.

So what can you take from these 25 great thinkers that will help you get the women you want? The take away is that dedication and persistence is the only way to make something happen and get results. These men created a system that helped them are productive in their work lives. I invite you to do the same in your dating life. For example, as part of your daily routine, incorporate approaching and interacting with five beautiful, interesting women each day. This does not mean they have to be into you or you have to get a phone number. It just means you have to push to approach and interact with them.

Reject Me Please!

Rejection sucks. It sucks for men. It sucks for women. It sucks for everyone. However, it sucks less when you experience it more. Honestly, I know that seems counter-intuitive but it is true. I know from my own personal experience that the more I put myself out there and feel the brunt of rejection, the less it affects me.

While listening to NPR one day, a story came on discussing torture victims. They said that those who experienced torture in their lives no longer felt fear. It is as if they hit their tipping point after being tortured and developed the belief system that nothing could be worse, so why be fearful. This made them push forward even harder and with more confidence. Think of the fear of rejection as a trial by fire; once you overcome it, you will conquer fear in other areas of your life as well.

I talk to hundreds of guys every week, thousands every month and they all fear the same thing: Rejection! Instead of putting themselves out there to be rejected, they do not do anything and get no results. In my opinion that is just silly. They are rejecting themselves, so that they will not experience being rejected by a woman.

A few days ago, I was responding to comments that people post on my blog and I stumbled across one that made me think, this guy gets it! This guy gets how to handle rejection by a woman and how to flip the switch so his response creates attraction.

This post honestly made my day! I love hearing when guys who read my materials finally get it and they stay grounded and calm. Very sexy and super attractive. Honestly there is nothing sexier than a man who is unaffected by my actions. Gives me chills just thinking about it. Why is this? Because it signals to me this man can handle things.

"I had this guy that I had stuck in the Friend Zone for years. Whenever he would bring up becoming something more, I would say, "No, I don't want to ruin our friendship," and he would crumble and try to convince me to be with him. Total turn off. Then one time when he brought it up, he said to me OK, smiled, and then stopped contacting me. That man has been my boyfriend for 2.5 years. Ha." —EMILY, 28.

Lesson: Rejection is not the bad thing; it is the way you handle it that can make you feel so horrible.

How Do I Motivate Myself to Go for It When I Know I'll Get Rejected?

Email:

Dear Marni,

Thanks for all this brilliant information. The way you devote your life to helping people fulfill their dreams is admirable. You are clearly a good person, I appreciate that. Perhaps you can help me too. My main two issues are lack of motivation and going for the kiss.

I often do not have the motivation and self-belief to be able to go up to any girl and talk to her. I always think of it as a pointless exercise, even when I know deep down, that if I apply my mind to it, I could do it.

Secondly, when it comes to going for the kiss, I have several issues. I initially think that she won't want to kiss me (even if she is attracted to me) and that she'll reject me, or laugh in my face, or play hard to get, or that I'll do it at the wrong time and I'll screw it up. Or I think that even if I do get the kiss, that sooner or later she'll just leave me for a guy who's cooler or smarter or more sexually experienced than me, and it's not worth the hurt that will all lead to.

Anything you can advise would be incredibly appreciated. Best wishes,

Joshua

My response:

Hey Josh,

Thank you for the kind words. It means a lot to me!

I think both of your questions get the same answer from me. It seems like you are not seizing the moment in all areas even though you know it is the solution. So let me ask you this, what is it that is really stopping you from going after what you want?

My belief and what I teach to every man that I work with is to remember you are allowed to ask for whatever you want as long as you are being honest, non-manipulative, and non-hurtful. This means, go approach any woman you want to talk to. Kiss a girl you want to kiss.

Marni

Five Steps to Eliminate Approach Anxiety

Want to eliminate approach anxiety and start dating amazing, beautiful women? Start dating the women you want instead of settling for the women you can get? Stop messing around and letting approach anxiety or lack of confidence get in the way of your success with women?

Here is what you are going to do:

- **Get Out of the House this Weekend**. I do not mean for two minutes. I mean for, at the minimum, four to five hours a day.

- **Interact with People**. Not just women, but people. This will open you up and prepare you for when a great woman comes along. There is too much pressure out there just to talk to women. Interactions mean saying hi or asking questions that you really want to know the answer to. The best is literally making an observation

To access FREE bonus materials go to:
http://winggirldatingtips.com/gih-bonuses/

about the world around you. Remember, you are not trying to squeeze your way into their world. You are showing them yours.

- **Talk to People**. No pick-up lines, routines, or tricks allowed. None of the "Hey I was just walking by and saw that you were a woman and so I thought... (Insert pick up line)." None of this Pick-Up Artist stuff.

  All women have heard these types of energy sucking approaches before and it comes across as, "I wanted to approach you but have no idea what to say and I'm not going to know what to say once I finish saying this sentence." It also says, "I'm boring, unoriginal and will be a horrible lover."

  I want you to talk to people with no outcome in mind. If they choose to respond, then great! However, your success is based on you engaging others. Anything other than that is a bonus. Talk to people as if you already know them. Avoid formalities like, "Hey, my name is X and I was standing across the park." Instead, say, "It's nice out today." Or, "That shirt is bright."

- **Practice Having Conversations**. The key to an amazing conversation is all about observing, listening, and sharing (responding with something interesting not just a question) which in turn leads to connecting. Conversation is all about building blocks. Observe something about a woman, then listen to their response and share your own experience. I talk about this in detail at:

http://www.winggirlmethod.com/get-insider-her-bonus

- **Engage and Disengage/Practice Leaving the Conversation**. I see so many men freak out thinking that as soon as they walk away from an interaction with a woman, one of the following will happen:

- Some other guy will swoop in and steal her away.

- The attraction and chemistry between them will disappear.

- She'll completely forget about him once he's gone.

   Honestly, if any of the above happens, then you never had a chance with her anyway. So do not be afraid to walk away. For now put a cap of one minute on all your interactions. Walking away is actually super attractive. It shows that you are not desperate, but self-confident.

   If it is a woman, you like and you have decided you want to get to know her better say something like, "It was great talking to you but I have to go. However, you are awesome and I would like to get to know you better. I would like to take you for coffee next weekend. Give me your number and we'll set it up." Get her number, then walk away.

How Can I Tell What a Woman's Eye Contact is Signaling?
Email:

Marni,

I stopped by the grocery store on my way home from work and I saw this girl walking toward me, we made eye contact, but half a second later, she looked away. When this happens, I find it even harder to approach a girl that catches my attention. When women make eye contact for half a second and then look away, does that mean she's not interested? Or maybe she is shy? Or maybe she is creeped out?

What is it? Should I approach?

Michael

My response:

Michael,

Think about it this way. If you look over at a hot girl and she looks back at you, what is your first reaction? The typical, gut reaction is to look away. Why? So you are not caught, right? Don't worry. I do that too.

I did it yesterday at the gym. I looked over and saw a guy I thought was attractive. He looked at me, so I quickly looked away. It's my automatic response because you are not supposed to stare. However, after I looked away and composed myself, I looked back at him and smiled calmly and confidently. He smiled back and we had a nice moment.

What I am getting at is do not be freaked out by being caught off guard. Compose yourself and then take your shot!

Marni

Are You Into This Girl?

A common thing I notice with all the men that I work with is that no matter how awesome they are, for some reason they forget to ask themselves the important question, "Do I even like this girl?" They are so wrapped up in attempting to make a woman like them that they forget to think about it from their own point of view.

Stop putting woman you have just met on a pedestal. Women are not unicorns with breasts. They are not mythical creatures that will disappear instantly if you look away or say the wrong thing. They are human beings, just like you!

The more you focus on making her like you the harder it becomes for a woman to become attracted to you. Why? Because you are not present, and therefore are not showing her your true self.

I have heard so many men say to me "In a first interaction, I don't want to say too much about me just in case she's not into what I say. Can't scare her off till she's hooked." To which I say you're wasting your time. A woman is never going to be hooked to someone who is bland and boring. Start talking and sharing yourself--if that rocks the boat, then you'll know that it wasn't a boat you should have been on in the first place.

The next time you approach a woman, ask yourself, "Am I into this girl?" If you are, great, ask her out. If not, excuse yourself and move on. Staying in the moment and keeping the control in your hands will help you avoid being nervous and trying too hard to impress her.

The next time you approach a random girl I want you to ask yourself the following questions:

- Do I find her interesting?
- Is she engaging me?
- Do I like her?
- Am I attracted to her?

Remember, this whole process of meeting people and approaching them is about finding someone who is right for you. It is not about making everyone like you.

How to Avoid Being Creepy

"Creepy" is a really negative term, but unfortunately it is one that women use often to describe guys.

The annoying thing is that the vast majority of guys branded 'creepy' are done so unfairly. The truth is they are usually cool, calm, confident men in every other aspect of their lives who just cannot seem to convey that to the women they meet. Luckily, a few indictors will help you never be wrongly labeled again.

1 **Eye Contact**. Eye contact is one of the most powerful ways we communicate who we are as a person. It tells a person if they can trust us, whether we think they are hot and how we feel about ourselves. Look away too much from a person and you will appear shy. Stare too heavily and you will come across as too intense. Avoid looking creepy by getting the balance of eye contact just right.

Here is a tip on what to think in your head while you make eye contact with a woman. Think this, "I know a secret about you. It may be good. It may be bad but you have no idea that I know it about you." This will help you soften your eyes and create an energy that is attractive rather than creepy.

2   **Persistence**. Persistence often pays off with women. Sometimes being direct and quick to say what you want works. However, there is a limit to this. Fill her inbox with messages, ring her phone off the hook, or show that you have too much of a strong emotional response to how she behaves and you will seem pissed-not persistent.

3   **Keep it Casual.** Before your relationship with a woman becomes a sexual one, it is best to keep the conversation casual rather than sexual. Sure, there is a time when you have to get your seductive mode on and be okay to whisper things into her ear, but being too sexual too early can be creepy. No woman likes to be cat-called walking down the street, and likewise she may not appreciate you making a comment about her breasts on a first date!

4   **Avoid Signs of Nerves**. Visible signs of nerves tell the people you are with you are not 100% comfortable in their company. If this happens, the fact that you are uncomfortable will also make them feel uncomfortable. So try to stop fidgeting, be calm, and if you are feeling nervous take a breather and remember she is just a person too.

To access FREE bonus materials go to:
http://winggirldatingtips.com/gih-bonuses/

5   **Avoid Lingering**. One of the most important things I teach is that you have to 'approach, approach, approach!' If you hesitate too long before hitting go, and wind up following a woman around a bar with your eyes, instead of just saying, "Hi," you will seem weird. So next time, do not 'hover' nearby hoping that she will say hi. Instead, take the initiative and strike up a conversation. This way you will seem confident and not creepy.

Follow these simple tips and I promise you will appear cooler, calmer, and more confident; qualities that women find seriously attractive.

3. Dating Online

How to Write a Female-Friendly Profile

Writing a profile should be easy, but for some reason people tend to over think them. The main thing to remember is that your profile is about you and what you want. It is supposed to represent the reason you are online.

1   Don't Write Really Long, Boring, Profiles

Most people think that longer is better. Ever heard of less is more? Well that applies to online profiles as well. Do not make it long just to make it long.

The Female POV:

I asked a few of my Wing Girls what it means when men write a really long detailed profile:

"A really long profile means either self-absorbed, needy (which is gross) or not that bright. A guy should be able to summarize who he is in two to three paragraphs or less."

—MARISA 34

"Does this guy have a life? Seems like he spent the past three months

of his life writing his profile. So not natural."

To access FREE bonus materials go to:
http://winggirldatingtips.com/gih-bonuses/

—MELISSA 29

"Too long means too short in other areas!"

—JODI 38

"If a man is really creative and actually has something to say in

his nine paragraph profile then I may find it interesting but

usually

I get bored after the first three to four paragraphs. If he can't

express who he is in the first few paragraphs there is something

fishy about him."

—EILEEN 42

"Too long is too much. I have read tons of online profiles and

the ones that get me are concise and to the point."

—JEN 26

Why write her a novel before she has decided to learn more about you? I call this throwing up on women. Men do this on and offline. It means you are throwing up everything about yourself and this is:

- Unattractive to women.

- Desperate.

- Disrespectful toward yourself.

- Needy.

- A big step towards online failure.

Please note that I am not saying that information about you is a turn off and will deter women from viewing your full profile. However, too much unneeded information is just that, unneeded.

2   Avoid Spelling Errors in Your Profile

I am not a grammar fanatic, nor am I a spellchecking freak. If you have read any of my materials, you will quickly realize that. However, spelling errors and obvious grammatical errors are a no-no. Your online profile is a representation of who you are. It is a commercial, your banner ad, your billboard in Times Square. So treat it as such. It is what you will use to get attention from amazing, attractive, intelligent women. So use it properly.

3   Make Sure You Have the Right Picture

We all know that when women are "window shopping" on online dating sites, the pictures are super important. Call it superficial or call it bitchy if you want but it is a reality. Your picture is the first thing a woman sees when checking out a profile. You have to make sure you select the proper pictures.

I am about to give you a great online dating tip for selecting a profile picture. This online dating tip came to me from one of my newsletter members, who I will refer to as X.

X, told me about a recent study done by OkCupid which discovered that women are more attracted to men who look away from the camera in their profile photos. I had never really given much thought to the position of a man's face in a picture, but after thinking about it, the study made complete sense. I have include my email correspondence with X in this chapter, X's results from his own private study, and my own commentary.

Email from X:

Hi Marni,

I wanted to tell you about an online dating experience I had which was incredibly fascinating...

For a number of years I have been doing the online dating thing. I have had profiles on Match, OkCupid, JDate, etc. In every one of these profiles, I posted photos with me looking directly at the camera.

After reading about a study done by OkCupid, which talked about how women are more attracted to men who look away from the camera (something about being more mysterious), I thought I'd give it a try.

Within two days of posting my looking-away photo on OkCupid (attached), I received 22 new visits to my profile. For many women, this is probably typical. For your average guy, not so much!

I was amazed at how a simple little profile tweak could make such an enormous difference. I continue to receive many more profile visits than I received previously.

I hope you find this useful.

X

X attached a picture of himself looking away from camera, which I have included here. My initial response when I saw this picture was "Hey! That guy is super cute. I would date him."

My response:

X,

This is fascinating. Thank you so much for sending this to me. Before I make my comments, I would love to see your old pictures so I can compare. Can you send me your old pic? To be honest, in this pic you look super cute and attractive. I can see why you got hits on your profile.

Marni

X's response:

Thanks Marni! I am attaching three of my older photos (pasted below). Feel free to use on the site. Glad you found the info useful.

My response:

First off, I want to say that you are still very cute but there is something somewhat sad about these three photos. I can totally understand why women are giving you more attention with the new picture. It is way more eye catching and really paints a picture of a moment with you. These three photos look forced, cheesy and to be honest, not so attractive. The other picture makes me want to know more about you.

I think the reason looking off gets more attention is because it feels like you are not trying as hard. Translation, I do not need your approval. It feels more real and comfortable. Photo 1 is in your face. It screams, "Look at me! Pick me, pick me!"

Looking away is subtler and not as aggressive. It makes it less obvious that you are participating in dating online. Thank you so much for sending these photos and allowing me to use them on my site. I know this example is a great online dating tip that other men can use.

X's response:

Thanks so much for your feedback. I think you hit the nail on the head about not trying as hard. This would be a great service you could offer profile photo critiques! I cannot believe I have been using these other photos for so many years. These dating sites (some of them) are a money pit, and look at how much money I could have saved by using a better photo. No regrets, but I see a lot of value in photo (and profile) feedback.

X

The point of the profile picture is to give women a snapshot of your life, not to show you in numerous uncomfortable and forced positions. I hate when people have professional headshots. Are you auditioning for a film or looking for a date? To help you out, I have put together a list of six rules for selecting an online dating picture. These rules are based on my own online dating experience as well as feedback from twenty other women.

Rules for Selecting Pictures

1   Do not have too many photos of you by yourself smiling (it looks unnatural and downright creepy.)

2   Have a friend take your picture. Pictures of guys holding the camera at an angle to take a shot just looks stupid. All women will see is a loser with big nostrils.

3   Include a mix of pictures. The picture section is for providing a snap shot into your life. A couple with

you and friends, a couple of you doing an activity, one with a pet if you have one.

4   Have 5-7 pictures max. You really do not need more than five pictures of yourself. Between five to seven is okay, but more than seven is overkill.

5   Choose recent pictures where you look good. You obviously want to show your best self, not the version from 1984 or the one where you haven't showered for a week or two.

6   Test different pictures and do your own study. Select a profile picture and post for one week. Reach out to twenty women and measure your results. Then do it again, with a different picture for four more weeks.

I guarantee that if you follow these rules you will instantly notice a difference in your online dating results.

Things to Include In Your Profile
In order for a profile to be truly complete and ridiculously attractive to women, it must:

- Include a clearly written and not confusing profile.

- Show charming character or personality.

- Display a range of interests and hobbies, as well as a range of knowledge.

- Show a balanced personality: someone confident but not cocky, someone passionate but not too sensitive, etc.

Avoid these pitfalls:

- Avoid including a run-on list of things you like, or making blanket statements about yourself. E.g., I like dogs. If you say I like dogs, use the magic word *because* to expand on why you like dogs. It will attach an emotion to what you are saying and will help a woman get a visual of you.

- Do not include any negatives. Yes, honesty is great, but you should not "spill the beans" in your personal ad.

- Do not "point out" any negatives and sound lighthearted about them. You are only going to demonstrate a lack of confidence and pull her attention towards that negative feature

- Do not include any sexual remarks, even as a joke. Be very careful with any jokes or attempted humor. If a woman does not know you yet, she will not understand that you are joking, especially online where tone and inflection are stripped away from what you write

These quick tips are meant to be guidelines for you as you go through creating your online profile. Make sure to go back to these tips once you have completed your profile.

How Do I Ask Her Out On Facebook?
Email:

Hey Marni,

Can you look at a message I want to send on Facebook. Tell me what you think.

"Hey silly, don't you know guys don't like being called handsome. Just kidding. Seriously, though, I'd like to hang out one of these days somewhere where we don't have to scream into each other's ears to communicate."

My reply:

That's great. Make what you want more specific and confident. Not "let's hang out sometime." Tell her what you can do to hang out. Do not be afraid to be direct and ask for what you want.

Marni

Follow-up:

How about this?

"Hey silly, don't you know guys don't like being called handsome. Just kidding... Seriously though, I want to go out and do something, like grab a drink or hit up a gun range. Hit me back with your number."

My reply:

Not something. Not sometime. Tell her when, how and what you want to do. The only way to get what you want is by asking for it!

Marni

Be succinct and have a definite plan.

III. How to Talk to Women and Create Attraction

"When a guy is too focused on "getting me" or "getting my attention"

I feel it instantly. Makes me pull back and put up barriers"

—*WING GIRL JEN*

As I said before, I do not believe in trying to be someone you are not. I do not like tricks. I do not like pick-up lines. They are disingenuous and impermanent. I believe in honesty. I believe in packaging oneself in the best possible way, in utilizing what you already have to attain optimal results. I believe in being the best version of yourself you can be. With honesty comes longevity.

Women do this every day of their lives. They put make-up on. They wear high heels and perfume. They have been taught how to enhance what God gave them. Men have a bit of a disadvantage in this department. Men have to be more themselves, (more natural), than women do. What you see is what you get, right? Wrong!

In this chapter, I will teach you how to enhance what God already gave you. Not by being deceptive. Not by being someone you are not. You will learn to value what is already good about you and amplify it.

Have You Heard About the Magic Line to Say to Women That Instantly Makes Them Drop Their Panties?

No? Because it doesn't freaking exist. For women, it is not about what you say; it is about how you say it. Honestly, I could have ten men stand in front of me and say the exact same line. One of them I am going to want to slap, one I may feel the need to coddle and take care of, one I may feel immediately turned on by and the rest I will feel nothing for.

Women do not give a shit about the words that come out of your mouth. At least not in the first ten seconds. They are attracted to how you feel. If you feel icky, needy, or nervous, there is no way we will want you. If you are calm, cool, collected, and confident, it gives you two more minutes of our time. This chapter is about how to talk to women, not in some sort of internal video game, but as another human being who you find attractive. First up, what do you talk to her about?

What Do I Talk to Women About?

Honestly, anything as long as they are included in the conversation. This is true as long as you actually are present in the conversation and not trying to get to an outcome. If you are outcome focused, you will not be in the moment with a woman and she will feel that instantly and put up her own barrier.

To access FREE bonus materials go to:
http://winggirldatingtips.com/gih-bonuses/

There is no wrong conversation to have with a woman, except maybe how you are a big fan of XXX rated porn. However, even that, with the right woman, may be a perfectly normal conversation. The thing is that you must stop thinking about what she wants to talk about. Think about what you want to talk about and go from there. No need to exhaust yourself attempting to be a mind-reader. Stick to what you know best: you.

Trust me; if you are past the age of three, you have endless hours of conversation inside you. All you need to do is bring it out and share it. Throughout your life, you have had many conversations, right? In fact, I am sure most of them have been very successful and even easy! That means you already have the skills and you are just freaking out because you think that conversation with women needs to be different. It doesn't! If anything, the more normal the conversation, the better. The excitement should come from within you, rather than the topic.

Tip: You had better start finding yourself interesting, because if you do not, a woman never will. This does not mean bragging or being arrogant. It means that you know you are awesome and have interesting things to share. The only thing you need to be careful of is that you are present in the conversation. That means that you listen, engage, and are present. Not off in dream land, fixating on whether or not she is into you or hoping that she says a certain thing so that you can reply a certain way. Focusing on outcome instantly removes you from the conversation.

There is no right thing to say to a woman. There is however, a right way to say it. It's all about what is behind the statement. I could have ten men lined up in front of me saying the exact same "Kiss Ass Tried and Tested" pickup line.

However, I will have a different reaction towards each man based on his presence and body language.

Women want to feel comfort, confidence, and strength in character when they are talking to a man. Here is an example of how to talk to women about anything you want and like!

Talking About Video Games

If you talk about video games, talk about the video game then talk about why you like video games. The 'why' is the important part to women because it carries an emotion, and emotions are what women look for in a conversation. Remember, women react to how you feel, not what you say.

Remember to inject emotion into a conversation by using the magic word, because. Another great phrase is, "Which means..." Both will force you to expand and elaborate on what you say to a woman. I like video games because it lets me be in a world so different from my own. I really like getting to lead and do things I would never do in my real life. Then to include her in the conversation you will say: "Do you have anything like that in your life that takes you away from your everyday routine?"

As long as you attach an emotion to a topic, are present, and remember to include her in the conversation, you have free range to talk about anything! To warm up your conversation tools, I have an assignment for you.

To help others, go to http://www.winggirlmethod.com/get-insider-her-bonus and post your questions on my blog. This

To access FREE bonus materials go to:
http://winggirldatingtips.com/gih-bonuses/

way you can get feedback and help others who may not be able to come up with questions.

Remember, these questions have to work for you. There is nothing wrong with a little preparation and mental rehearsal. There is however, something wrong with avoiding the approach because you think you have nothing to say. I guarantee you will see different results than you have ever seen before including: Women becoming more attached to you, women opening up more to you, and women wanting to see you again.

How to Compliment a Woman Correctly

I received a fantastic email from a guy asking me about the right way to compliment a woman.

He asked:

Have you done a blog on giving compliments? I think I may have seen something that touched on this but I ask because of something that happened at work recently. A woman I work with asked me if I complimented women very much as I tried to pick them up. I told her that I rarely do this. She told me that I was wrong for not doing so. I disagree but what are your thoughts?

Al

My response:

Your friend is kind of right. I wish she had given you more direction because simply complimenting for no reason can actually hurt you with women. From my experience, and the thousands of interviews I have done with women from around the world, I know that. It's about where the compliment comes from, not about what is said.

So before complimenting, ask yourself these questions:

- *Am I complimenting to get something? - If your answer is yes, then do not compliment.*

- *Am I complimenting to fill space so that there is no silence - If your answer is yes, then do not compliment.*

- *Am I complimenting because I do not know what else to say - If your answer is yes, then do not compliment.*

- *Am I complimenting so that I can stay in conversation - If your answer is yes, then do not compliment.*

- *Am I complimenting to make her like me more - If your answer is yes, then do not compliment.*

Compliments need to be real in order for them to have an impact. If they are fluffy or dishonest, we will disregard them and they will have no effect. We can smell bullshit from a mile away. Not sure if you saw my article on the magic word, but words have no meaning to women if they do not have an emotion attached to them. Which means a compliment must be deeper in order to get a response from a woman. She has to feel the compliment.

For example, "You are beautiful."

As nice as this compliment is, it means nothing.

Here is the response this will get from a woman:

To access FREE bonus materials go to:
http://winggirldatingtips.com/gih-bonuses/

"Great. You are the fifth guy to tell me that today. It's nice to hear, but is that all you've got?"

It's not really said that bitchy, but I am trying to show you the effect it has, even if it is subconscious. Picture this response as a simple shrug and a smile, which means that these words have no emotional impact.

Here is a better way to compliment if you want to say you are beautiful, "I know most men can see you're a good-looking woman, but I think your real beauty shows once you start to speak."

Now that statement shows a woman that you see her, and you get her true beauty.

Notes: Compliments still have to be sincere, even if they are said in this manner.

I have an exercise for you so that you can truly understand how it feels to woman to have an empty compliment thrown her way. Ask a stranger to compliment you for 30 seconds straight. Preferably a man. I know this seems silly but it's actually fun. After, I want you to tell me how it felt to have empty, meaningless compliments thrown at you by another person.

The answer is exactly how women feel when you compliment them for no reason! So next time when you ask yourself, should I compliment her? You will have all the information you need to make a proper decision.

To that end, let's take a closer look at how to stay out of the interview mode most men fall into and actually start connecting to women.

Get Out Of Interview Mode and Start Connecting

The reason you are shoved into the Friend Zone or categorized as "Mr. Nice Guy" is that you do not know how to get out of interview mode! How do you even begin to get out of interview mode, especially when you cannot think of things to say? First, make a rule for yourself. The rule being that you will not ask more than two questions in a row (of a woman). Once you hit question number two, that should be a signal to you that it is time to share.

For example:

"So are you from here?"

"No. I'm actually from Toronto."

"Really?"

"Yes. I grew up there, but moved to LA when I was 23."

That's two questions. Therefore, it is time to share or make a statement. Here is what not to do:

"What did you move here for?"

Even writing this out I can hear the energy being sucked out of any girl you are talking to as she silently starts to plan her exit strategy.

Here is what you should do:

"That's a pretty gutsy move. I have never been to Toronto but I hear it is an amazing city. Do you go back there often?"

That's how you do it.

Check out this email that I got from Michael. He is one of my clients that I work with over Skype. Over the past year, he has gone from the wimpy guy women cannot stand to the attractive guy that women are crazy about. He finally gets the importance of chemistry and connection and why it causes women to feel attraction.

Email:

Hey Marni,

Here is another update, and an insight about connection. It is amazing how often so many of us go through life (and online dating especially) in what I call "interview mode."

By "interview mode," I mean that we answer questions as if we are on a job interview with answers that are crafted to "sound cool," be socially acceptable, and politically correct so that the other person will like and accept us.

Everyone who does online dating "loves their job" and "had a great weekend with their friends (because people like them, dammit!)" The ironic thing is that we can subconsciously pick up when others are dealing with us in "interview mode," and when that is the case, we do not feel much connection and chemistry with the other person.

I used to do this a lot on dates. I still do it more than I am proud of. It has gotten me labeled as a Nice Guy (no chemistry).

My experiment: I am going to catch myself whenever I go into "interview mode, "and say something that is edgy or truly on my mind, no matter how politically incorrect it might sound.

"I like my job, but I sometimes fantasize about leaving to become a porn star." "I spent the weekend writing a paper for work…Yes, I am proudly in touch with my nerd side. I'll be visiting friends in San Diego next weekend."

"You look amazing, and I'm asking about that ring on your finger because I want to hold your hand."

I know we talked about this before, but I am finally seeing the concept that we discussed in a new light and I want to share this with you.

Cheers, Mike

My response:

I love it. I hope you have realized why interview mode pushes you into Friend Zone or Mr. No Second Date. And why doing everything you said in your email creates chemistry and connection.

It is because when you are in interview mode, you do not give women anything to latch onto. They walk away knowing a hell of a lot about themselves but nothing about you. So why would she ever think about you or want to see you again? You were just a dude who wasted five minutes of her life collecting data for a survey.

Moving beyond "interview mode" is where connection happens.

When a guy is stuck in "interview mode," on some level a woman may be questioning the guy's sincerity. Instead of thinking, "this guy is great." She is thinking, "What does this guy want from me? Why is asking questions? Get to the point, buddy!"

Love that this is all starting to click for you!

Marni

Why Women Need to Feel You

Women absolutely want men to come up to them and make them feel something.

Let me explain:

I got started thinking about this with a Facebook comment and the ensuing thread it generated:

> *"Wanna know a secret? Girls want you to talk to them! Trust me I know."*

Tons of readers responded back with positive responses like, "Hell yeah!" or, "Don't share our secrets Marni, and then one guy started to make negative comments like this one:

"That is, if they allow the guy to approach them without writing them off or wondering, "Just what does he want from me..."If the guy can fathom all these hurdles, the girl might tolerate conversation."

I am not opposed to negative comments because that is where and when we all get a chance to learn. If we all agree with one another, we never learn anything new. However, this one got the rest of my Facebook fans going before I even had a chance to respond. I wanted to share one of the amazing comments left after this negative statement that clearly explains women. I have to admit, I could not have said it better myself.

Comment:

"X, you seem like a super intelligent man and often that intellect can work against you. You are looking for linear logic and consistency because in the world of academia what is said and written means everything.

What a woman says is close to meaningless, and consistency is irrelevant. It does not make them bad; it is in fact what we absolutely love about them. Emotions are everything. To reconcile the seeming inconsistency between the two statements replace the word 'talk' or 'think' with 'feel'.

Women absolutely crave men to come up to them and make them feel something. Talking is just one mechanism to do that, so is picking her up and spinning her around, so is kissing her, so is the tone of your voice, so is what you wear and how you look (to a much lesser extent of course). Feelings are everything.

"What do you want from me?" is social conditioning that all men want is sex, that they will use you up and spit you out. That they will lie to you to get what they want etc. You counter that by demonstrating a willingness to enjoy the moment without preconceived notions.

The moment you ask about her job and clearly do not care about the answer and are not enjoying the moment, it becomes apparent you are there for ulterior motives. That ulterior motive has no soul and no feeling and nothing good will come of it for either of you even if you did get sex. All feelings come from the moment.

We love women by how connected to feelings they are. It's okay that their words don't always reflect reality, they are far better at spotting liars and unsafe people than men ever will. Get in touch with your heart man, watch some Oprah and cry over the kids in Africa, watch the original Pride and Prejudice and feel yourself get swept away with the awesomeness of Mr. Darcy, you'll start to feel it." This in a nutshell, is women!

Again, could not have said it better myself.

How Do You Make Women Feel You?

So how do you talk to women so that they feel you? Believe it or not, most of the time women do not give a shit what you say. They care about what they hear! Am I confusing you yet? One thing you must know about women is that we do not think, we feel. In addition, we feel everything. If you want to successfully talk to a woman, it is essential to talk to her on all levels, rather than just with your words.

The way you talk is vital to creating attraction: it tells her what you have as a man, suggests your lifestyle, and talks volumes about your compatibility. Remember, women are subconsciously evaluating you on multiple levels. It's not just your pretty face that keeps them listening.

Talking to women can be hard to master. To be great at talking to women, you have to talk to a woman, as a woman would. You have to leave your logical, factual tone in the boardroom and connect with her emotionally or you will lose a woman's interest every time.

As an experiment, pick up any girly magazine and look at the language that is used. The words are more expressive, painting pictures rather than announcing facts. In order to successfully talk to women you need to make them feel something, rather than think something about you.

Now I know that I have said a million times, there are no magic tricks when it comes to women, but I do have one magic word. The word does not guarantee you get laid, but it does guarantee you will inject emotion into your conversation.

The magic word is: because.

By adding "because" to your conversations you will be forced to get more descriptive and detailed. It is the difference between:

"I like football."

And:

"I like football because it is the one time when I could get all my friends together in one room. We all have our own lives now and it's nice to know we still have something that brings up together."

Boom! I literally leaned closer and closer to the computer as I typed that sentence. Any time you say the word because you cannot help but expand and provide an internal thought (emotion). By expanding how you talk, by using 'because' women will find that they can talk to you more easily. This means they will talk to you in more detail, and in return, you can paint them a picture of your lifestyle.

Talking to women as a pro is like muscle training; to solicit this level of attraction, you will need to do some training.

To access FREE bonus materials go to:
http://winggirldatingtips.com/gih-bonuses/

How to Make Decisions in 60 Seconds Or Less

"A man who can make a decision in a split second,

especially when under pressure, is the sexiest thing to me."

—CARLY, 27

"When a man can't make an important decision, I think to myself,

what do I even need you for? I know it's harsh but it's what I think."

—JENNIFER, 31

"I have had several first dates with men where they pick me up and say 'so what do you want to do.' Those are the first dates that also become the last date."

—LESLEY, 26

Women love men who are decisive and can make decisions easily. It is the defining quality of a true man. Whether it's where to go on the first few dates, what show to watch on TV or how to pack up your apartment on moving day, decision-making is a must have skill for any man who wants to attract and keep a woman interested.

Have you ever wanted to make a decision in 60 seconds or less? You only need one tool to pull it off and here it is:

First, let me acknowledge that decisions are tough. Most of the big ones - the ones that scare the crap out of you - are related to big unknowns. Case in point: entering or leaving a relationship. How you react when faced with a super big decision like this will define you as a person.

Most people freeze when faced with the unknown. It does not matter if your current situation is awful - you are afraid of the alternative. Yeah, sitting on the couch every Friday night watching reruns of the Simpsons and eating cold leftovers is an awful prospect, but what if you are rejected repeatedly? That's even worse...or is it? Here's the thing - I cannot tell you if a decision will make your life better or worse, but I can tell you that nothing will ever change if you refuse to make any decisions at all. Here is a very simple, easy to use method for making decisions fast.

Most of the time, you will evaluate and decide in less than 60 seconds.

Are you ready, because here it is:

Every time you are faced with an alternative, ask yourself, "Is this really me?" You are not worrying about what happens to you, but whether the path you choose is a good reflection of who you are. Stop thinking of decisions as major world-shaking events, and think of them as a form of self-expression.

Decisions are so much easier when you think of them as an extension of yourself. It does not matter if the path is a pain in the ass; if you know a decision is the perfect representation of you, it is much easier to make. On the flip side, sometimes a decision leans heavily one way but you know deep down that it is not you.

The beautiful woman across the room who somehow isn't right for you? Follow your path of self-expression. Here's the hard part. On one hand, you want to evaluate the options and choose one based on your personality and needs. Is she right for you? Yes? Then, it's time to act.

Making the decision is not the same as acting on it, and often, people allow their fear of acting to stop them from even making the decision. Separate them. Make your decision completely separate from the act itself. Maybe you will wait a day or two. Maybe you won't. The courage to act on it - that comes later.

If you cannot figure out whether a woman you have just met at the grocery store is right for you, sit down and ask yourself some basic questions. How does she make you feel? What does she have that you are looking for? Stop worrying about making her happy and ask whether this is the woman that you want in your life. It is amazing how different this will make the decision process.

One quick thing to mention - when you ask yourself if a woman is for you, this is the ideal you, not the guy who cannot get out of the house on Friday night. This is the very best self you can put forward, the one you fantasize of being. When you are living your perfect life, is this woman for you?

That's the question you need to ask yourself; do not hold yourself back. The coolest thing about this method? It works in nearly every aspect of your life. You're going to use it a lot when deciding whether to call her back or go on a second date, but it can be useful in just about everything else to.

How to Get a Girl's Number in Less Than 30 Seconds
So many men that I speak to think that there are specific rules to follow when it comes to asking for a girl's phone number. I am here to tell you there are not. There are no rules, no guidelines, and no right or wrong time to ask for a phone number. Actually, that's a lie. There is one rule.

Ask for a girl's phone number when you decide you want it.

Below is an email from one of my coaching clients, updating me on a recent success story. I gave him an assignment where he had to pick up a woman and get her number in less than two minutes. He wrote to tell me he was able to pull it off in less than 30 seconds. Amazing! My commentary is after his email.

Email:

Hey Marni,

Just wanted to keep you up to date on things with a story from Starbucks yesterday. I was in a meeting with a man and a woman, and looked up to see a young woman walking towards us, heading for the doors. She looked at me with a bit of a smile and had her head slightly tilted to the side. I held her gaze, excused myself, immediately got up and walked directly towards her.

Without skipping a beat I said, "Hi, listen, I'm in a meeting right now, but I'd love to grab a coffee with you some time." She looked a little stunned, but held eye contact. She then said, "Sure, okay!" I pulled out my iPhone, hit the contacts button, pressed new, and said, "Do you know how to work this?

Just put in your name and number." She did, I told her I had to get back to my meeting, and she left. The whole process took about thirty seconds from open to close and is a new record for me.

I returned to the table, the couple looked at me with a bit of disbelief, and we carried on with our meeting. I couldn't help but notice the woman kept checking me out after seeing me number close with X, and shifted her body language to face me directly. And, forgive my candor, but I caught her doing a package glance a couple times, and she kept on just looking at me with that slow up and down gaze. She also remained distracted for the rest of the meeting, and seemed to have her mind elsewhere.

The man was clearly stunned by my action with X and had that "Did that just happen?" look on his face for the rest of the meeting. Fifteen minutes later, I texted X with, "Hey you." She responded immediately with, "Hi! Thanks for the text" I replied, "First ones free..."

Now the only drawback is she is young, early twenties (again) so I don't really know where to go with this. Still a little bizarre how easy it is for me at 43 to meet women that young. It is satisfying at some level, but rational me realizes it is an untenable situation. Anyhow, just wanted to share this with you.

(Client)

My commentary:

First of all, amazing! Right? Second, as a woman, I am not surprised by this at all. What my client did was proactive, masculine, and super attractive.

- Saw a woman he was interested in.

- Approached her.

- Asked her for what he wanted (her phone number).

- Got back to his life.

Done!

The reason why it was appealing to the woman he approached was because it was exciting and it made her feel special. Let me take a moment to explain the latter. I know other male experts (PUA's) will scream, "Making her feel special is the kiss of death," but there is a huge difference between making her feel special and pouncing on her.

> **Special**: Means that you acknowledge that you have a life, you respect yourself, and you are choosing to allocate some of your time for a selected female.

> **Pouncing**: Means that you have forgotten about yourself, lost all emotional control and need that woman's approval.

My client made this woman feel special and not pounced on. That is why she responded by giving him her phone number. It is also the reason that the other woman, with whom he was having his meeting suddenly found herself wanting him to notice her. She wanted to feel special too!

If you see a woman you want, approach her, ask for her number, and then get back to your life. In and out. Do not worry about "the right" thing to say, worry about what happens when you do not say anything at all.

To access FREE bonus materials go to:
http://winggirldatingtips.com/gih-bonuses/

You have no idea how many opportunities you are missing out on every day. There are tons of women around you at all times and the only reason they are ignoring you is that you are letting them. I guarantee, if you can do this assignment three times a week for one month, you too will be able to succeed in getting a girls number in less than 30 seconds!

Special Bonus for You

I have been doing this for a very long time and I find that there are some resources that speak for themselves. Because you have taken such a monumental step in improving yourself and learning how to create instant attraction with the women you meet, I want to provide you with some of the tools I provide my clients for free.

Just visit the link listed below and you can access my guidebook on how to have conversations with women and create instant attraction. I am also throwing a handful of video examples on this special landing page just for readers of this book - the next time you are at your computer, make sure to check these out!

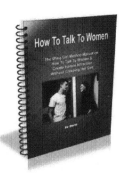

http://www.winggirlmethod.com/get-insider-her-bonus

How to Juggle Multiple Women

Email:

Hi Marni,

I have two women that I am dating and cannot decide which one to settle down with. I have dated them for a few months now, finding them equally serious potential for a long-term relationship. Neither knows of the other I do not think.

Although it is driving me nuts, I refuse to let one go because I do not want to make a mistake and let the wrong one go. Obviously, I will eventually pick one. In the meantime, do you have any advice on keeping them without losing one or possibly both?

Greg

My response:

My guess is that each of these women is gradually building a connection to you and it is not fair to lead them on for too long. Two to three months max, but after that it is time to man up and make some decisions. Shit or get off the pot, right?

First, I would take a few days to write down what you want. Keep them out of it for the moment. Really think about what you are looking for in a partner and please do not start listing, "I want a woman who plays tennis and has huge boobs and a good smile." You are looking for a partner, not a masturbatory visual.

Things like:

- I want a woman who respects the fact that I require XYZ.

- I want a woman who cares about others.

- I want a woman who values religion, faith, spirituality etc.

- I want a woman who wants children, loves children.

- I want a woman who is loyal.

- I want a woman who can laugh when things get tough.

- I want a woman who is independent, has her own life, her own friends.

- I want a woman who is a great communicator.

Then once you know what you want. Talk to them and see what they want. All you need is more information so that you can make a decision. You do not need to make it alone. However, no more of this stringing-along shit! Not cool, and if you let it go on for much longer, you will most likely lose both of them.

IV. The Dating Playbook

Why Isn't Dating Fun Anymore?

I think there was an email sent to all the single people in the world telling them that dating can no longer be fun. At least that's what it seems like.

Everyone I know that is single and dating is miserable. All my friends, my neighbors, my clients, everyone! Now, if you are one of these people who did receive the email, I am writing this because I want you to know something - dating is fun! Why else would you want to participate in it if it's not at least a little fun?

I think one reason the fun of dating dwindles is that people put a lot of pressure on what they think they want rather than actually focusing on what they want. This limits their options and makes connections impossible.

I recently had a conversation with Dr. Benjamin Karney from the Relationship Institute at UCLA (Karney, 2012), who told me about a psychological study performed to see if an individual's pre-determined list of qualities a partner must possess hold up as a measurement of what they really want.

They decided to perform this study using a speed-dating environment where an equal number of men and women were present. Prior to speed dating, they asked all participants to list what they wanted most in a partner. As a whole, men said looks were the most important to them and women said earning potential was most valued.

When the speed dating commenced, they asked everyone to rate each person on an attraction scale, and on an earnings potential scale, with 10 being the most attractive or top earning potential and one being the lowest. You would think that at the end of the session the men who said looks were the most important would have connected with the women they rated as a 10 for looks. You would also think that the women would feel a connection with the men, which they rated as 10 for earning potential.

Not so.

They found that each participant's pre-determined list of qualities had nothing to do with their selection of those that they felt a connection with. Interesting right? This means that the list of "qualities" they had been using to select possible dating partners was bubcus! (That means rubbish for those of you who do not speak Yiddish.)

These lists of qualities are possibly limiting people from meeting their potential mates. Even worse, they are stopping people from finding fun in the dating process because they may be adding too much rigidity to their selection phase. If you are one of these people, then I have a challenge for you:

Go out for the next week with an open mind. Do not pre-judge a person before interacting with them. Do not use the list of "qualities" that you usually go by. Give them five minutes to see if there is a connection. If not, leave.

Another challenge is for those who are dating online. Do not write off a person because of the list of qualities they are seeking. Again, qualities are simply boundaries that people impose on themselves. Push those boundaries and go after what you want. Enlarge your dating pool to the size of an ocean. It's time to start making dating fun again.

1. How to Get a Date

A Case Study: How to Correctly Ask a Woman Out

I have many guy friends. Guy friends who I love and think are the best guys in the world. Moreover, guy friends who can still shock me when I see how terribly they handle themselves with women. Lucky for my guy friends, they have me to get female advice from.

I was on the phone the other night with one of my guy friends talking about girls, sex, attraction, love, and past relationships and he told me about this girl he had been interested in a long time ago in college that he happened to see by his office that day. He said that he always regretted not asking her out in college and that he was not going to let this opportunity pass by him again.

Therefore, he did some recon work and got her email address. I told him to show me his email before sending it to her. Thank goodness, he showed me because it would have been disaster had he sent it. Our email correspondence is below along with my commentary on how to ask out a girl properly:

Email from friend:

Hey X,

We never actually speak when we see each other, and I think we should change that. Let me know if you want to grab a coffee or a drink sometime.

Y (my friend)

My response:

Did you send this yet? Please say you didn't. It's sweet but it has no oomph to it to get a girl riled up. It can be stronger and more attractive. Seems a little soft. Again, it is good but it can be better. Women are at their peak of attraction when they have the opportunity to feel their most feminine.

My friend's email was not terrible; it was nice, which in some ways is worse.

There was nothing to latch onto. No excitement but sweet. You want to offer a woman something that she has no choice but to say yes to. Not because she was forced to say yes, but because she was intrigued and excited.

Friend's response:

I could just say:

Hey X,

Would you like to meet for a coffee one day?

However, I put in the other filler and formality because she doesn't actually know me. The opening summer stuff is there as polite throat clearing before moving on to the point.

Y (my friend)

To access FREE bonus materials go to:
http://winggirldatingtips.com/gih-bonuses/

My response:

Do not be polite. Also, say what you want. Try it that way. I find that when guys are trying to "be polite" they end up coming off as saps, wimps, or suck ups. No good, not attractive and does not get the reaction you are looking for from a woman. The more masculine and direct you can be with a woman the better. This does not mean be a jerk, an asshole etc.

Friend's response:

X,

Got the wave in the Path last week, but we never actually speak when we see each other.

Let's change that!

Do you have time for a coffee or a drink this week? I am free Thursday or Friday mornings.

Y (my friend)

My response:

So much better. Love the "let's change that" part but get rid of the exclamation point. Needs one more tweak, but getting there. Does it feel better to you? Try, "I want" as part of what you say. I want to get to know you better, I want to take you out, or I want to change that.

In the beginning stages of dating, it is about you. What you want, what you are looking for. You do not know her yet, so the person to take care of is you. Therefore, do not be ashamed or fear that you are being too obvious with what you are asking for. Being direct and honest will always get you the best results.

You want to date her. You want to sleep with her. You want to go for coffee. So say it. Say what you want.

Friend's response:

Got the wave in the Path last week, but we never actually speak when we see each other. I want to change that.

What days are you free this week to grab a coffee? Thursday and Friday morning is best for me.

Y

My response:

Love this! Send.

Friend's response:

Subject: I Owe You One

This is what she wrote back to me 10 minutes after I sent:

Hey Y,

Yes, the Path seems to be such a social place these days! I am always running into familiar faces. I would be down for a coffee break this week - any day but Thursday works for me!

Friend's response:

Ok great, let's do Friday. I had to run out of the office this afternoon and only just got home. I will tell you about it Friday, but it will likely make tomorrow super busy for me.

Are you able to get away 2:30 Friday?

I feel bad because I did not get her email until just now which is four hours after she wrote.

Should I just write tomorrow?

My response:

No! I hope you didn't send that. You are pouncing, throwing up on her. You can tell her about your great day when you see her. In response to your last comment, you have a life, you are busy, and you work hard. Not all your energy needs to shift direction for this girl.

You will get back to her when you get a chance to. Wait until tomorrow and write a direct email saying you will meet her at XYZ at this time. Done. Direct equals sexy. Lots of words and fluff equals future of her crying on your shoulder about other guys. Get my point?

The first email my friend wrote to this girl may have gotten a response; it may have even gotten him a date. However, it was not attractive and it certainly would not excite her. What it would do is slightly interest a woman and get her to say, "Might as well." Is that what you want? For a woman to agree to go out thinking, "I'll give him shot. He seems nice" is not enough.

You want a woman to say, "Oh my God, I want this guy and I can't believe he is giving me his attention! I am excited to go out with him." That is exactly what this new email will do. It will make a woman excited and feel butterflies in her stomach.

How to Be Direct and Ask Her Out

In my opinion, there is only one way to ask a girl out. Before I tell you the one way to ask a girl out, I am going to tell you a few ways that you should never ask a girl out.

"I was thinking that maybe sometime you and I could go somewhere"

This is indirect, shows lack of confidence and is not specific. Staring at or watching a woman for a week then finally working up the courage to approach her, say hi, have friendly conversation, walk away, and wait for three more weeks of this before you feel she is comfortable enough with you to let you ask her out-- this is creepy.

Talking to a woman, being flirty, funny, and attractive and waiting for the next time you see each other to ask her out. This is stupid and does nothing more than frustrate her.

In my opinion, all of the above are big no-no's and will not get you anywhere with a woman. Why? Because each of them shows a woman, she is of higher value than you, more masculine, and in complete control of the situation. You don't want that, right? I know you don't.

Here is a little secret about women that will help you put your mind at ease the next time you want to ask out a girl.

Secret: Women Want to Be Asked Out

However, they want to be asked out by a man who they believe has value. Now value does not mean money, power, strength, or any other superficial characteristic you assume women want. A man who has value is a man with self-

To access FREE bonus materials go to:
http://winggirldatingtips.com/gih-bonuses/

respect, a life of his own, and the ability to ask for what he wants without the fear of rejection.

So how do you present yourself as a man of value? You use the method I am about to share with you every time you interact with a woman and ask her out. The number one way to ask a girl out is to ask her directly for what you want.

Being direct and asking for what you want without fear of being turned down is the sexiest, most attractive way you can ask a girl out. Trust me! I am a woman and I know. The men in my life who have been indirect with me always got an indirect response. Meaning I wavered, flaked, and canceled because I did not find them to be men of value.

I know that asking for what you want may be a bit of a challenge. From the men I have coached over the years I have heard several reasons why, "Asking for what you want with women" was not an option for them.

Reasons like:

- If I ask her for what I want she will know I like her.

What exactly would be wrong with that?

- If I am too direct, she will think I am an asshole and I don't want to be.

Being direct does not mean you are an asshole unless you act like one. I am not telling you to hit her over the head, tell her she is fat, and then ask her out.

- I feel uncomfortable being that direct. I think it's rude.

It is even ruder to waste a woman's time and energy by tiptoeing around what you want. Do you know how much energy is wasted when women are nice to guys who cannot just spit it out and ask for what they want?

Here is an exercise to prepare you for the next time you have an opportunity to be direct with a woman and ask her out:

During this time, even if you do not have an answer for something, fake it and select one. I want you to experience how it feels to be in command, owning your decisions. This is something I talk about in great depth in my program, "How to Become a Man Women Want." So many men miss amazing opportunities with women. This means so many women miss out on great men. That, in my eyes, is a tragedy.

I want you to do this exercise to practice and understand that you are a man of great value that every woman would be happy to meet and have the chance to go out with.

Are You Coming On Too Strong? How to Avoid Being Overeager

I wanted to share an email I got from someone recently. I am sharing it because I know that the situation this guy is in, may be something you could encounter in the future or may be dealing with right now. I'm honestly not sure how to classify this situation other than calling it overeager. I see many

To access FREE bonus materials go to:
http://winggirldatingtips.com/gih-bonuses/

guys make a situation into something much bigger than it is because they are worried of either:

- Falling into the Friend Zone

- Losing the girl

- Messing up

This is what ends up happening because they are overeager. Funny how that works right? Read this guy's email because I know you will learn something from his situation as well as my advice for him.

Hi Marni,

I just signed up for the Wing Girl program and am looking forward to learning how to be a better man. Thanks! I did have some questions regarding someone who I am currently talking to. First, a little background information: I'm a single guy in my mid-thirties. I live in Los Angeles, but work takes me to San Francisco every other month for a week at a time. On my last trip, I met this girl and we went for drinks on a Thursday night.

Everything went well and we decided to meet for dinner the next night. Dinner the next night got off to a bad start because I was late. She was pissed. I tried to make the best of it, but it was miserable. I kept asking why she was so upset and halfway through she started opening up about herself and her past. She had abusive parents and a rough time in High School where she got into drug and alcohol use. She also mentioned many bad relationships with unreliable guys. At the end of the night, we hugged, said we would stay in touch, and said goodbye.

I left for Los Angeles the next day. A month has gone by and we are emailing each other. I'm trying to keep it light and casual, while avoiding the Friend Zone. I will be back in SF in January and will try to see her then.

Anyway, I know this is a lot, but you can give me your advice and thoughts.

Sincerely,

X

Here are his questions, and my words of advice:

Question one: What do you make of her past? Should I be concerned? All the articles on AskMen say I should run away as fast as possible.

My answer:

You should run away if you are getting huge red flags about her. Are the emails fun or are you just sending them to stay in touch and make sure she is still there. I would say an email every other week would be enough. You guys did not kiss or anything when you hung out in San Francisco, so it is still not anything solid yet. I would keep is casual until you get back to San Francisco. Plus, its holiday time so enjoy this time for yourself, send her a happy holiday's message that's cute and kind of teasing and then contact her in January.

Question two: Not sure how I feel about past drug use, guys, etc. How do I bring up the topic of STDs and when?

My answer:

That's an individual thing. I know it's not my ideal either but I also know I adjust if I like someone. My husband was a much bigger drinker than I ever imagined myself with and I had a hard time adjusting to it because I wanted to change him but when I stopped trying to change him and just accepted it, he actually started drinking less. I'm happy I stuck around!

Question 3: She is religious. I'm not, but it doesn't bother her. Is there anything I should be concerned about?

My answer:

Concerned? No. I would hold off on all these concerns for now and just really think about whether or not you like her. Seems like a lot of thought and effort going into someone.

Question 4: Is this part time in San Francisco lifestyle fair to her or to me? Is it workable?

Marni's answer:

Same response as before. Do not worry about fair. You guys are pen pals for now, so take a breath and do not take this so seriously

Question 5: How can I keep emailing her interesting? How do I start flirting or is that a bad idea?

Marni's answer:

Of course, you should flirt! Why else are you emailing!

Dating can be a hassle if you are not invested in having a good time. That is why I want to show you a few of the emails I have received from men who are so close (and in some cases so far). Remember, dating is supposed to be fun, so take the advice below and use it to relax and enjoy yourself, not create new stress.

Do I Need to Have a Full Conversation With a Woman Before Asking Her Out?
Email:

Hey Marni

Just wanted to say you doing a great job and I love all the advice that you have been giving us guys.

I have a quick question for you. The other day I was waiting for my train and I saw this hot girl sitting down waiting for her train also so I went and sat next to her and a few seconds later our train arrived. I didn't get to talk to her. The thing is I could tell she could have been a little interested. She even came and sat next me on the train.

My question is what would she or any woman do, for that matter, if I gave her my number and said, "hi I would love to chat with you sometime but I have to get off at the next stop?" Would a woman call even after not having a conversation, and just handing her your number?

Thanks

N

My response:

No, no, no! Next time you have an opportunity like this get it on! She sat next to you on the train. Oh my God, it was as if she was saying to you please pay attention to me. If she had no interest in you, she would have made sure to sit far away from you, seeing as you made the first move by sitting next to her.

Generally, any time you see a woman you like, or even ones you do not like, start talking to them. If you like them then say, "Listen, I'm getting off at next stop but give me your number. I want to take you out for xxx." If you do not get the chance to talk to them but want that chance, then say the same thing.

You can meet women anywhere and you are always allowed to talk to any woman you like. You do not need permission other than the permission you give to yourself. You are also allowed to ask out any woman you like even if you have not spoken to her for a long time. No limitations. Let the woman take care of the rejecting instead of you rejecting yourself.

Do not let an opportunity like this pass by you again or I will hunt you down!

Marni, Your Personal Wing Gir

How Do I Ask a Woman On a Second Date?
Email:

Hi Marni,

I would like to know how you get second dates. Should I wait for the girl to suggest that we should see each other again? Because I have read that advice from other dating experts. Is it okay to say, "I would like to do this or that. Do you want to come with me?" Or something like that?

Carlo

My response:

Carlo,

Of course, you can ask for second dates if you want to go on them. I do not agree with getting her to ask you because most women will not ask you and therefore you lose out. Lead! As the man, always lead. The more you lead, the more a woman will be inclined to follow. Why? Because when you lead and take on the masculine role, it allows a woman to fall into the feminine role. That is what women want-- to feel feminine.

I actually just did a great interview with a good friend's new boyfriend. While she and I were hanging out, she told me that the way her new BF would end each date and ask for the next one was super attractive. She said, "I had no choice but to say yes to his invite. It was direct, confident, and attractive."

Here's how he would end each date: "X, I had a great time with you. Then recalled something from the date that he liked learning about her and said it. I would like to take you on Wednesday for dinner/movie/walk. Are you free?" The reason why it was so attractive was because he was stating what he wanted and then relayed that information to my friend. The response to that question is yes or no. Clean cut!

Try it,

Marni

Is Okay to Date on a Casual Level?
Email:

Hi Marni!

My name is Leslie. I'm a 47-year-old black guy. Divorced, three kids, two of which are living with me, helping them make the transition into adulthood. With my hectic schedule, I have realized I cannot really give a long-term relationship the time it needs (hence the end of my two year relationship last week). How do I date women knowing this?

Very Respectfully,

Leslie

My response:

Leslie,

You are asking me if it is okay to date multiple women and explore them on a semi casual basis. Correct? I am all for exploring your options and creating a life that is fun, exciting and works for you. However, once you start involving others it can become tricky because your wants may not coincide with their wants. As a note, this can even happen when both people have similar end goals.

Therefore, my advice to you is to be honest with tact. This does not mean telling a woman on the first date "Hey, I just want to let you know that I don't want anything serious and just want to have sex and fun." It means, not leading a woman down a path that is false so that you can get what you want.

As long as you are being honest through your actions and not promising things that may give false hope, you are free to do whatever you want.

Number one rule: As long as you are not hurting, misleading, or being dishonest, you are allowed to do and ask for whatever you want.

Marni

Do I Tell a Woman I'm Dating Other Women?
Email:

(Anonymous)

If I see this woman again, should I let her know I am dating other women or just keep it to myself?

My response:

Not unless she asks, and if she asks do not say, "Yep, four; sleeping with two." Be discreet about it. It's your life and your information but you have to respect her. So say something like, "I am dating and trying to figure out what I want. Having said that, I am really enjoying my time with you and look forward to getting to know more about you."

Marni

2. How to Rock the Date

"I hate it when guys won't plan a date and expect me

to make all the decisions. Especially in the first few dates"

—SARA 29

Okay, so you have met the woman. You have attracted her. You have succeeded. Now it's time to date.

Fact: Women call their female friends after dates. Every woman does this. I have been the caller and the answerer. Many times. Many, many times.

There are things all women want on dates. There are questions all friends ask after dates. I am going to tell you what they are, why they are, and how to get a rave review. I am also going to go through the dating process - the calling, the messaging, the intimacy, the whole damn circus. Anxious yet? Good. Your future date is too.

Eleven Mistakes Men Make on Dates

The first date is one of the most important for obvious reasons. The better you do on the first date the more likely there will be a second and third to follow. I asked a bunch of my female friends to think long and hard about the men they have dated in the past and the errors they made that turned them off. After lots of discussion, I have put together a list of eleven mistakes men make on dates. I am not even going to try to fancy it up for you because I want the messages to be loud and clear.

Please, read it carefully, and do not make these mistakes!

1   **Arrive In a Car Full of Junk**. This should be a no-brainer, and yet it happens repeatedly. I remember a date whose steering wheel was spattered with what looked like dry white paint. The guy explained that it was because every time he drank milk, he sneezed.

2   **Fail to Take the Lead**. There is nothing worse than being picked for a first date and the guy turns to you and says. So what should we do? I know this sounds bitchy that women want the first few dates to fall on your shoulders, but too bad. It's how it is. This does not mean you have to work for weeks planning elaborate dates for women but it does mean that you should have something prepared, even if it is a simple walk around the block to get to know one another better. Women love leaders. Start leading on your dates and you notice a huge difference in the way women respond to you.

3   **Choose a Bad Restaurant or Venue**. One big tip that I give to guys is to pick a date location that makes you comfortable. It will help put you at ease because you will be comfortable and familiar with the situation.

To access FREE bonus materials go to:
http://winggirldatingtips.com/gih-bonuses/

4   **Be Rude to Others**. Nothing is a bigger turn off then a guy who is a prick to others but nice to me. I will admit that some women do get off on that but the majority are not fans. One thing women are looking for is consistency. It's nice if you open the door for her but if you let it slam on the elderly woman behind you, it will send a red flag to your date that what you are showing her is not really who you are.

5   **Name Drop or Brag about Accomplishments**. If a woman likes you, she likes you for who you are. You do not need to make flimsy connections between yourself and Bruce Willis's ex-nutritionist to get a date's attention. Talk instead about what you enjoy doing, and what you have done recently that is slightly out of the ordinary (river rafting, wine country tours, etc.). Having said that do not hold back on sharing information about who you are. If you had lunch with the president last week, tell her. However, do not tell her for the sole purpose of impressing her.

6   **Forget to Ask Questions and Listen When She Responds**. This should be a simple one to follow. Conversation on a date should be like a nice ballroom dance. There are two people on the date so do not forget to ask her questions. Most importantly, do not forget to let her know you have heard what she has said. For every question you ask a woman that she answers, listen to her response. Then add to it. Let her know she has been heard and her words have not been wasted.

7   **Speak Ill of Past Dates, Girlfriends, or Wives**. It does not matter how astoundingly unpleasant your

ex was, your current date does not want to know about it. She will instantly put herself in your ex's shoes and feel some female solidarity. Therefore, dissing your ex is dissing all women, which is dissing your date. Got it?

8   **Ogle Other Women or Watch TV**. Do not ogle. I mean, if Angelina Jolie walks by, you are not expected to ignore her. However, your expression when you return to your date should be of bemusement or confusion, not unfettered lust! Moreover, if your team is playing on the TV at the pub, please do not watch it. Please. (Note that this suggestion can be ignored if your date is a fan. In that case, you have hit the jackpot. Change seats, order a pitcher, and enjoy the game!)

When my husband was dating, he used to make sure that his back was always to the restaurant. This helped keep him from searching for me while he was on dates with others.

9   **Be a Debby Downer**. Talking about our woes and complaints can be very easy for someone, but on a date, a woman does not want to hear about it, especially on a first date. She wants to hear that you are a positive man that will always be able to keep her safe and se-cure no matter what happens. So, be sure to always put a positive spin on whatever sad story you tell. It shows her that you have a positive outlook and can handle whatever comes your way.

10   **Agree to Split the Tab**. If you asked her out, you pay. Even if you did not ask her out, you pay. Do

not let her trick you either by offering to pay her share. To avoid having huge credit card bills each month, make sure to select dates that do not cost a lot. Walks, drinks, coffee, art museums, etc.

11   **Not Try for a Kiss Goodnight or More...** Yes, you should try for a kiss. There are many ways to signal a desire to give a peck. You can ask, "May I kiss you good night?" It might work. If she says, "No," just smile and thank her for a great evening. If she says, "Yes," take it one-step at a time. Failure to at least try for something is going to make you look like a wimp, or worse, make her think you do not like her. So risk rejection and make a little move. She will appreciate it if she is into you, and if she is not, well, you will find out fast!

Above all, remember that women are people too. However, things that please your manly friends (noisy bars, bodily noises, wisecracks about other women) do not generally work on us. I hope you can put these eleven rules in play and have a good first date!

Where to Take a Girl on a Date

So, if number three on the list of eleven mistakes is choosing a bad restaurant or venue, what counts as a good option for a date? In fact, tons of men ask me, "Where should I take a girl on a date?" My answer to them is always the same, "Where do you want to go on a date?" The dating process is all about seeing if two people can connect and fit into each other's lives. Therefore, I feel that in the early stages I feel it is important to stay true to yourself so she gets an honest impression of your world.

Bring her into your world and see if she can handle it! A lot of men try too hard to figure out what would impress her, what would she want to do? Or, what will make her want to be with me more? Remember, in the beginning, you do not know this woman - she is no one to you. At least not anyone whose needs come before yours, right? So, stop focusing on her and start focusing on yourself. If you want to go to a salsa class, take her with you. If you want to go to a comedy show and laugh, take her with you.

A first date does not need to be extravagant, expensive, and showy. It has to be real and it has to be you. In fact, I strongly suggest keeping the first date short and sweet with the potential to extend. I do not want you to invest hours of your precious time (that you could be using to meet other women) on someone you quickly know you have no potential with.

How to Bring Up Sticky Topics: Kids, Divorce, Health, etc.
You may worry that a woman will discount you because you have bad skin, a job that causes you to work nights, or because you are a single father. This isn't true! Luckily, for guys, women rarely write a guy off based solely on his physical appearance or for one deal breaker in his life. Women are different from men in this way. Guys can be very set in a physical type that they have; whilst women evaluate the men they meet on a number of different requirements.

When you approach a woman of course they will think about how you look, but they will also measure up your general vibe - what you're wearing, what you say, how you present yourself, whether you make them laugh, what they know about your character etc. That is already a big list and it doesn't stop there!

You may now be worrying that it is impossible to pick up a woman if they are looking for so many things. Actually, it is just the opposite!

Even if you think, you have something counting against you during your initial approach, (maybe you have a small build and are after a girl who so far has only dated guys from the football team). That hurdle can be overcome if you present other aspects of yourself positively.

I'm not going to lie to you. Some women are superficial so they may not initially be attracted to you if you are not their type; or they may be concerned if you do not have the job or family situation that they would ideally like. However, the easiest way to stop them from judging you on that one thing is to demonstrate all of the other great qualities you have going for you. If you walk up to her worrying that because you are not dressed smartly, she will not give you a chance, then she probably won't.

Instead, I want you to say, "Fuck it, I know I'm a great guy" and go after her anyway! Having this positive attitude, this charisma, this belief that she will get it, will make it very difficult for her not to turn around and say the same thing back, "Fuck it, let's see what this guy is all about!"

Seriously!

Even if you have got a little something that makes it slightly tougher to meet women, you can still make it work by presenting all the other great qualities you have. Stand up, be counted, and put yourself out there. This is the way you will get the women you want to give you a chance. I am sure you know that when she gets to know you, she will like you more and more. So do not sweat the small stuff!

Still unconvinced? Then let me tell you a quick story.

When I was single, I went on several dates with men who had children. Some women will like the fact you have kids, others won't. Whether it is a deal breaker or not though will depend on how you tell them. Most guys I dated who had kids made a huge deal out of when they announced that they had kids. They made it so dramatic, as if I was going to flip out. They would say things like:

"I have to tell you something that I should have been honest about before. I have a kid but I really want to live my life still and I want you to be a part of it."

Because they made it out to be such a huge deal, I was caught up in the emotion of it and allowed this one potential negative to influence how I felt about the guy as a whole. Not just because he had kids but also because he presented a negative view of himself to me.

Then I went out with the other guy who casually mentioned he had a daughter and how being a dad made him an even better guy. "I freaking' love my daughter. She's what makes me wake up in the morning, but more importantly she's helped me be smarter about the people I let into my life." He then flashed a small smile at me that made me melt before returning to our conversation. See how different the tone was between the first example and the second?

With the second guy, I did not care that he had a kid. In fact, I was literally jumping out of my seat, excited and ready to be a step mom. He used what could have been a deal breaker to show me a whole bunch of other qualities about him that were so attractive. He can remain grounded, has a strong character, and is a great dad!

I want you to apply the same mentality to whatever you think is holding you back when you first meet women.

I want you to think:

"I've got it, so what, I know I'm an awesome guy and she's going to recognize that."

Write this down on a piece of paper and stick it in your back pocket. For two weeks, before you go out and approach women, look at it, then stick it back in your pants. Go in with this attitude, it is going to be so attractive that any small negatives will be blown away by the great qualities you have demonstrated. Put yourself out there, be positive and she will feel attracted to you.

Should Men Pay for the First Date?
This is just one of many emails, texts, and calls I have gotten on this topic. Men are constantly wondering if they need to pay for both of them on the first date - this email in particular resonated because of the results of the date:

Email:

Dear Marni,

I was told never to pay for a girl on our first date, but I took out this gorgeous blonde the other night, and I am wondering if she is not returning my calls because we went Dutch.

Thanks,

Dutch Boy, 28

Sydney, Australia

How you handle this is a huge part of how this date will end for you. Trust me; you want to get this right. I strongly disagree with much of what other people say about this.

Here is my response to this email:

Dutch Boy,

I will tell you, as a woman I feel that only a real man will pay for the first date; boys will offer to go Dutch. I know that tons of other male experts scream and preach that men should not pay because they feel it sets a man up to be the cash cow for the remainder of the relationship. I am a woman and I aggressively disagree.

If a man asks me out on a first date and then offers to go Dutch or holds out for me to offer to pay, it is so over. On that first date I want to feel like a lady and I want the man I am with to be a gentleman.

Listen, I know that others have used this tactic on women and it has been successful for them. Meaning they get laid after, but I will tell you why it works and when it will work, and then you can decide if that is what you want to get involved in.

I do have to say that in my opinion this tactic is cruel, manipulative, and usually done by an insecure man. Men that I would never want to introduce to my female friends and men that I feel should not be reading my newsletters.

From a female point of view, if the date is going well and she is into a guy she is thinking, "This is a great guy. I am attracted to him. I want him to kiss me at the end of the night and call me for another date." Then when the bill comes and he asks her to throw in cash she thinks, "Oh my God, what did I do? Does he not like me?" This puts the female in a very insecure space where she feels she must win him over again and therefore will do things she would not normally do to win back his approval.

Again, this is a negative space for both a man and a woman. Truth is she may sleep with you but will feel horrible about herself afterward and possibly ashamed. She will not return your calls and any plans are lost.

Not good, especially if you were hoping to continue dating her.

I want to be clear and let you know that I am not saying you have to take a woman out to an elaborate meal and wine and dine her, and then cover the whole night. What I am telling you is that a gentlemen who asks a woman on a date, will take care of the bill and let a woman feel feminine.

When I feel feminine, I feel alive, relaxed, and happy. A man who allows me to feel feminine is my hero! The sexiest thing is when a man plans a date, leads the whole time and then says, "Don't worry, I got it." This is the ultimate manly thing to do! Makes me melt just thinking about it. I always feel bad or uncomfortable with the man paying. However, I would be very disappointed if a man expected me to pay or made me pay on the first date.

The only time it may be acceptable is when I ask a man out. This is because it was my invite and therefore my responsibility to handle the bill. Oh how sexy would he be if he paid anyway! Now of course some of you are reading this and may still be thinking, "Money hungry bitch."

I know you are. I have many of my clients use this term and I want to put a stop to it right now. A situation like this has nothing to do with money; it has to do with roles.

Here are some other thoughts that may race through my mind if a man did not pay for a date:

"Is this even a date?"

"Does he just want to sleep with me?"

"Is he a jerk?"

"Can he take care of me?"

"Can he take care of himself?"

"Can I count on him?"

"Is he gay?"

"Is he cheap?"

"Is he driven?'

"Is he a loser?"

To access FREE bonus materials go to:
http://winggirldatingtips.com/gih-bonuses/

Again, this brings out insecurity or, in a stronger woman, complete distaste. When a woman expects the first date to be taken care of by the man it is not because she is only interested in his money. It is because she is looking for a man that knows how to respect and treat a woman.

Again, in my opinion the first few dates should always be taken care of by the man. Now having said that, a tip for men is that they should take notice of how a woman is acting during the whole bill fiasco. Does she offer to pay or does she look like she expects someone to purchase her meal? If the woman you are with just sits with no reaction then you are with the wrong women. She may turn out to be money hungry, a gold digger, or someone that a great guy with character should not be with. This spells trouble for the future and I would get out while you still can.

Once you are past the first few dates it means you have entered a new phase, the dating phase. Once you are dating the rules change a little because this is when both people start to become real. Things are revealed on both sides. The woman you are dating may have more money than you may or she may have less.

The men that I began dating in the past have been a mix. Some have more than I do and some have had less and therefore we paid for things accordingly. For example, with the men who had more than I did, I would buy breakfasts and he would buy dinners. We both contributed financially in the way that we could.

The guys I dated never felt taken advantage of and I never felt that I was spending beyond my means to impress. I would also offer to cook meals or do other things that may have not been equal to buying an expensive meal but the sentiment was there. That is all that you really should be looking for. It has nothing to do with financials it has to do with how much effort the other person is putting in.

Before you jump to the conclusion that you are financially being taken advantage of, you have to ask yourself a couple of questions. How much is she able to contribute and is she making an effort in other areas? No effort at all spells disaster. If she is going to take advantage of you now she is always going to take advantage of you. Nice girls will work with you and do not take you for granted or take advantage of you.

My advice is to spend what you feel comfortable with. If you end up in a situation where you feel you are being taken advantage of financially, politely say something. Communication is respectable. Only you can control whether or not the woman you are dating sees you as the cash cow. It is up to you to put up boundaries, set limits and take control.

How Can I Tell if She Likes Me?
Email:

Hi can you help me with a situation. There is a girl at the place I work.

Our eyes met and she blushed. Since then there has been something between us but I don't know what. I have clocked out for her at the end of the day and she seems happy for me to do this. However, she only allowed me to do this once. She has winked at me and she has checked me out. She has also looked at me when I enter the room. At the end of the day, I say bye and she responds but she does not initiate anything.

A. What is she doing?

B. What can I do?

Yours, Dave

My response:

Dave,

Answer to B: You can ask her out!

Answer to A: She is living her life and being friendly to a co-worker.

From the actions you describe, it sounds like you may be creating this connection in your head. There is no indication that she is into you but there is also no indication that she is not into you. See what I am saying? If you are waiting for her to pounce on you, it is not going to happen. If you want something, you have to go for it. Especially when it comes to women. Women, even successful women in business, still want to be feminine.

Right now, you are playing it safe with her. You are taking little steps to "test" if she likes you but in reality, you are actually just protecting yourself. Do not worry about it; we all do. As the famous Wayne Gretsky says, "You miss 100% of the shots you never take." So start taking shots. Again, if you want her, go after her. Be masculine, be a leader, and tell her you want to take her out.

P.S. No more punching her card for her!

Marni

Signs That She Wants to Be Kissed & Signs That She Doesn't

Ah, that moment in the evening when you and your date finally test the physical chemistry between you—a.k.a. the first kiss. The setting is perfect, you have laughed and talked, maybe had a few drinks and some good food. Everything is mellow and romantic. You lean in. Further. Further. Your lips meet—air? On the other hand, only slightly better the smooth cheek of your lady friend. You pull back in surprise. Her eyes are shuttered, her smile embarrassed.

What happened? She laughed at your exploding pig joke, came back from the bathroom rather than sneaking out the side door, and agreed with your opinion that Triple H really needs to retire.

Well, two explanations ultimately lead to the same situation:

1   She did not feel an attraction to you that would warrant a kiss

2   She did not yet feel comfortable enough with you

In either case, you have been shut down and are unsure why, right? The most likely reason is that you missed the all-important come-hither signals that women give out to let men know they want to be wooed. You missed The Kissing Code.

Here is a breakdown of the language a woman uses when she is ready and wanting to be kissed:

To access FREE bonus materials go to:
http://winggirldatingtips.com/gih-bonuses/

Signal 1: Her eyes are softened and slightly narrowed—this is the dreamy expression and she keeps dropping her gaze to look at your mouth. This indicates that she is imagining her lips locked with yours.

Signal 2: If she is licking or lightly biting her lips a lot (especially in combination with the first point) it means she is making sure they are soft and pliable.

Signal 3: What your parents told you was true: If a girl hits you, it is because she likes you. Gentle slaps on the arm or leg, and seemingly casual touches to your face or hands all hint at her desire to be close.

Signal 4: Listen to her voice. If it dips in tone and becomes slightly breathy the woman is inviting you into her personal space for a secret.

Now that we have covered ways to tell when a woman does want to be kissed, let's briefly look at warning signs that tell you she does not want to be kissed.

Warning Sign 1: When a woman avoids making eye contact with you, pay attention. It could mean she is just shy and nervous. However, if she looks around the room or over your shoulder she probably wants to be elsewhere.

Warning Sign 2: If your date purses her lips frequently—compresses them so they are very thin or even disappear—she could be displaying irritation, boredom, or impatience (none of which are harbingers of an impending lip lock).

Warning Sign 3: Keep an eye on her overall body carriage. Is she tense and circumspect with her arms and torso? When a woman keeps her arms folded, holds her hands in her lap, or hugs her arms around the chest she is attempting to make herself as small as possible to avoid contact.

Warning Sign 4: As for her conversation, a woman is not interested in a kiss if she purposefully steers talk away from anything personal or intimate. She will speak in a normal voice and keep a fair amount of distance between her body and yours.

If you still cannot seem to decipher The Kissing Code your date is using, settle for a kiss on the cheek, but linger near her face for a moment and allow her to make the choice of taking it a step further. When all else fails, just ask her if she would mind a little lip dancing.

Here are a few extra tips for you to keep in mind before you go in for that kiss:

1   **Don't Surprise Her**. Want to know why women occasionally duck and weave away from a kiss? It's because they didn't see that one coming. If you are not close to a woman, making good eye contact and speaking seductively, you are doing nothing to communicate that a kiss is coming her way. Try to make out with her out of the blue and she will react with shock, not pleasant surprise. In addition, you will miss all the fantastic anticipation we feel as women, when we know that a kiss is coming.

2   **Don't Use Cheesy Lines**. Another great reason for communicating that you want to kiss a woman through your body language and eye contact, is that you get to avoid those cringe worthy chat up lines. Lines like, "How would you rate yourself as a kisser?" just make my skin crawl! Kissing is natural; you do not need to use a line to initiate it.

3 **Take It Slow**. Kissing is an incredibly sensuous act for women and is amazing foreplay. It also gives us a little hint about how we might get on with you as lovers. Just like how you would not dive straight into sex, without the foreplay, you also want to take your time with a kiss. Start slowly and gently, then gradually build up to a more passionate kiss.

Here's a secret move you can do: Before going in for the kiss, get close to her, softly stroke the side of her upper arm while making eye contact and then make a triangle with your eyes from one eye to the next and then to her lips. You must have built a connection with her for this to work.

4 **Touch Her**: When a woman kisses a guy she will start to feel turned on; you want to make the most of this by gently touching her at the same time as you kiss her. Again, rather than grabbing her, or rushing things, it is good to start slow: she will let you know how far she wants to go. So do not just keep your arms glued to your sides: embrace her, stroke her arms, run your fingers through her hair, and give her a super sensory experience.

5 **Make Her Feel Comfortable**. After the kiss has ended, take a moment to pause, smile, and relax. If it is a first kiss in a public place, you may want to switch back to 'normal' conversation and take some more time to get to know her. Let her know that you are not just pushing for one thing and that you are into her as a person. Remember, the more relaxed and happy you are, the more she will feel the same.

Follow these tips, and while you may not have an Oscar-worthy first kiss every time, you are more likely to get another one!

What Should I Do When A Woman Flakes On Me?
Email:

Hey Marni,

My name is Matt.

Let's get to the question: I have known this girl for about 14 years (since eighth grade pretty much). We used to hang out all the time but I never made a move on her, even though I wanted to.

Eventually she ended up dating another guy for a few years. We lost touch after high school for a little while and then a few years back reunited and see each other every so often around town. I asked her to go with me to a wedding last year about 3 months before it happened so we could RSVP. She said yes and even found out that her sister and her best friend would be bartending at the wedding so we would be hooked up if it were cash bar.

Then finally two hours before the wedding she texts me and says she is not feeling good and cannot make it! Then later that night my date and I went out to the bar and she was sitting there having a drink with some people from work! She saw me and kind of turned away when I walked by. I didn't say anything to her and sat on the patio outside.

I waited for a little while and Jamie walked out and told me that her friends forced her to go out and drive them around. I was a little pissed off to say the least so all I really said was, "I'm glad you're feeling better" somewhat sarcastically.

So now a year later a mutual friend of ours from high school is getting married on Friday and I asked Jamie to go with me about a month or two ago and she said yes. She wasn't invited originally so she has to be a plus one to get in. There will be a ton of our friends there and I am kind of regretting asking her to go with me. Everyone is telling me I should not take her because of what she did to me last year. Just wondering why she did not come to the first wedding and should I blow her off for the next one? Thanks!

Matt

My response:

Matt,

This girl is not into you, so let's get that out of the way. If she were, she would not have disrespected you and then blatantly shoved her disrespect in your face. Did she apologize or even acknowledge her behavior? I hope so because if not then she is no good in my book.

Please keep in mind that I am not saying X is mean, or a bitch. I am saying she is immature or uncomfortable and this led to her selfish, hurtful behavior. X was not able to give you an honest answer. She had no guts to properly say no to the date and then didn't respect you enough to apologize for her actions. Again, no good.

Which leads me to, why would you want to ask her out again? Think about it? Now you can stand up and realize what happened last year or you can relive the same situation again. I would say be strong, be a man, and show her how confident, strong people handle things. My advice is to call her up and calmly tell her that you are going to need to break your plans with her and hope she understands. No need to explain.

If you do want to explain you can say that last year's situation left a bad taste in your mouth and that you respect yourself too much to put yourself in that situation again. Reliability and honesty are very important to you and she showed that she had neither. Your re-invite was a lapse in your judgment.

If you are able to express this to her calmly and comfortably it will actually drive her crazy, she will doubt herself, and she'll actually become very attracted to you. I swear! In the future, if someone does this to you and you find yourself in a similar situation, here is what you should do when you see your ex-date sitting at the bar after telling you she was sick four hours earlier: You walk up and say, "Can I talk to you for a minute." Then you lead her away from the group. You do not yell at her or act immaturely sarcastic but you let her know that you are the leader and that her actions disappointed you. You frown on childish behavior. Do not say this, but imply it with your tone. Be firm but kind.

You tell her, "In the future, if you get yourself into situations you don't want to be in, just be honest with people, and tell them. Dishonesty is not an attractive quality." That's all you have to say.

Note: She has absolutely no respect for you seeing that she showed up to the event. As long as you stay composed and know in your head that her actions were childish, you can feel proud that you did not invest more time in her. So again, cancel this date with her. Do not be mean, or rude or spiteful. Just let her know it is not what you want anymore.

To access FREE bonus materials go to:
http://winggirldatingtips.com/gih-bonuses/

Marni

Did I Ruin My Chances by Getting Too Cute Too Soon?
Email:

Hey Marni,

If it is okay, may I ask you a question about a situation specifically, if there is any way to recover from this? I met a girl at Whole Foods last week. We have been trying to make plans to meet up for lunch and with her moving into her new place and things being hectic for her, and myself going home for the week to see my family, we agreed that it would have to be sometime the next week.

Anyway, I think I got too cute on a text (sent this morning): "Hey how do you like your new place? Are your stuffed animals on the bed unpacked yet? Yes, even though you are this strong athletic girl, I can totally picture you keeping at least one stuffed animal..."

I didn't hear back from her, and I am a little concerned that my attempt to be funny might have been too much. She is a tomboy, and she admitted when we met that she swears when she drives.

Nevertheless, she does seem somewhat feminine underneath. She also said it was hectic setting things up with the move. So maybe this text was off. My plan is to call her Sunday night. How does that sound?

Meanwhile, I hope you are well!

Mike

My response:

Mike,

I will be honest with you. The text was a little creepy. The joke was not conveyed properly and it gave me an icky feeling. The text seemed a little premature and too cutesy to be texting to a girl you just met. It sounded like a boyfriend/girlfriend text. However, from a new guy it is just creepy.

In the future, think before you text and think to yourself, am I texting to actually say something or am I texting to make sure she doesn't forget about me. Texts that come from that "I hope she doesn't forget about me" place always fail unless she is already into you.

The one thing to point out is that you guys had already said you were going to talk/hang out next week. Therefore, there was no need to contact her. If you wanted to be sweet, you could have sent a simple text saying something like, "So how did the move go?" or, "Successful move?" or, "Enjoying your new place?"

If there was a connection with this girl, she should be able to shake the text and move forward to actually meeting you. Make sure you pull back a little and understand that just because a girl is into you and accepts an invite does not mean she is your girlfriend.

Marni

Should I Call or Text after a Date?
Email:

Hey Marni,

I have a question on calling the next day after a date. I met this great woman and had a great time with her. At the end of the night, she hugged me and said that she never kisses on the first date, I gave her a few kisses on the cheek, and she gave me a few back. I got a great vibe off the whole thing, I am confident that it was not a cop out and we talked about seeing each other again.

I want to text/call her and tell her that I had a great time and set up the second date. I am thinking that I should highlight some of the things that were great in getting to know her on the date and then take the same approach of the first date and tell her I want to see her again and give an agenda for the second date. Does this make sense? Should I call or text? Any advice you have here will be golden as always!

I hope all is well, and I look forward to hearing from you! Take Care,

Randall

My response:

Hey!

My belief system is that you can do whatever you want, as long as you are doing it with the right intentions. So, if the reason you are texting or calling is to calm you, then do not do it. If it's to make her think you are "nice," don't do it. However, if you genuinely want to text her to say you had a great time, do it!

Leave it at that. Say you had a great time and it was great discovering her addiction to gummy bears. Something cute.

Alternatively, if you had a strong connection and talked on a deeper level, let her know you find it refreshing to meet a woman who does XYZ. After dates, I want you to take time for yourself to process, get back to your life and then you can reach out again to set up another date.

A good statement to use: "I had a great time with you, and would like to take you out again next week. Are you free Wednesday?"

It's a hard statement to say no to. It's direct, it's clear, and it's confident.

Marni

Ten Reasons Why Being Unhealthy Can Affect Your Dating Life
This is something we need to address because your appearance and general health can have a huge impact on your ability to meet and date women. Even if you kill it in the approach, you may not have the energy, level of attraction, or follow through to show her a good time if you don't take care of yourself. That Krispy Kreme may look innocent, but think again. Being unfit and out of shape can have a detrimental effect on your dating life.

From the dates you go on to your confidence both in and out of the bedroom, how fit you feel will affect your love life. If you still cannot see the link between hitting the gym and hitting on gorgeous women, here are my top ten ways that being unfit or unhealthy effects your dating life.

1   **Dating Is Tiring!** Even if you do not lead a 'Sex and the City' inspired love life, dating takes time and

To access FREE bonus materials go to:
http://winggirldatingtips.com/gih-bonuses/

energy. Rushing out to dinner after work, long nights spent wide-awake laughing and kissing, are exhilarating but also exhausting! Make sure you have the fitness level to burn the candle at every end during the honeymoon period.

2   **Dating Involves Activities**. Whether you want to swing by a salsa class, go for a bike ride in the park or take a long stroll across the beach, some seriously romantic dates also require you to be active. Get fit and do not limit yourself to a night out at the movies.

3   **Dating Involves Dining**. Of course, the classic date is over dinner: Not brilliant if you feel self-conscious about ordering that lobster mac and cheese due to your waistline. Do not restrict where you can go to eat, or feel guilty when you get there; hit the gym pre-dinner and work up an appetite.

4   **Dating Means Approaching**. Before you get to go on any of these amazing dates, though, you need to meet the people to date. Walking up to the cute woman at the bar is not always the easiest thing in the world, especially if you feel self-conscious. Boosting your BPM will also mean a boost to your self-esteem and give you the confidence to say "Hi."

5   **Dating Means Choice**. Dating is all about exploring different people, and finding someone who is a great fit for you. You do not just want a woman who you find attractive: you want a girl who is fun, smart and totally gets your impersonation of Steve Carroll. Do not limit the kind of women you think you can approach, by having poor self-esteem. Get fit, get

confident, and go for the women you really want: not just the ones you think you can get.

6   **Dating Means Dress Code**. Just like how you do not want to restrict the women who you think you can approach, or the dates you can go on, you also want to be able to wear clothes that are both stylish and appropriate. In fact, you want to feel sexy: so that means getting to a fitness level where you are happy to wear a well-tailored suit, feel great in a pair of swimming trunks, and amazing in the nude.

7   **Dating Means First Impressions**. Just how you would not walk into a job interview unprepared and ungroomed, you want to go out to a date feeling as if you are presenting your best self to the world. So do not look back to your high school photo and wish you still looked that good; present yourself at your fittest, and happiest, today.

8   **Dating Thinks Sexy**. Yep going on a date with someone means that you are both considering a physical relationship with each other. If you go into this sexually charged environment feeling self-conscious, then you will not feel sexy. Moreover, if you do not find yourself sexy, how is anyone else going to find you sexy?

9   **Dating Feels Sexy**. At least it should do. The problem with poor fitness and diet is that it significantly dings your immunity and your libido. So despite the candlelit dinner, red wine, and gorgeous woman, you may just not really feel like it. This would be a big shame!

To access FREE bonus materials go to:
http://winggirldatingtips.com/gih-bonuses/

10   **Dating Is Sexy**. A few great dates should end up with you being able to form an electric sexual connection with someone. Being unfit may mean that your nights of passion do not last as long as you would like though. Having great sex is not just awesome for your health either, the endorphin releases also means you will feel happier all the way through to the morning after the amazing night be-fore. Therefore, if it came down to a choice between a doughnut and dating, or a mid-afternoon sugar fix and sex, I know which one I would choose!

V. How to Avoid the Friend Zone

Urban Legend: The Man Who Went From Friend to Lover Just by Waiting

Have you ever heard the story about the wimpy guy who was in love with a girl for two years? Well what happened was this. He focused so much attention on this girl, listened to her complain about boyfriends, went shopping with her, was her shoulder to cry on and was there for her whenever she needed him. He was so focused on one girl that he totally ignored other potential women because he was sure one day she would come around.

Well, turns about that she did! Moreover, he didn't even have to say anything. One day the girl turned to him and said, "Oh my God, why hadn't I ever noticed you before. You are exactly the man I want and have always needed. I love you and want to have sex with you every day to make up for lost time."

You want to know why you have never heard this story before? Because, it did not happen and never will. That is not how women work and using this semi manipulative tactic of back routing to attraction will always fail. Do not ask to be a friend if what you want is to get busy. Ask to get busy.

The Difference Between a Friend and a Lover

I have an exercise for you. A guy that wrote into me asking about the Friend Zone and how to get out of it inspired this one. I told him that the only one who is responsible for you being in the Friend Zone is you. Then I gave him an assignment.

I told him to write me two lists. One list is a list of characteristics of a friend. The other is a list of characteristics of a lover. I told him that once he wrote the list it would be obvious to him where he was going wrong.

Here is his list:

Characteristics of a friend:

1   Trustfulness

2   Can talk to during times of emotional needs

3   Be there for personal advice and personal support

4   Can talk about anything together

5   Fiercely Loyal

6   Defend my friends no matter what the odds or the

enemy

7   Regularly staying in contact

8   Defending my friends' names

9   Willing to talk anytime when your friend is in trouble

10   Do anything for your friend

11   Defends friend's honor

12   Forgiving

Characteristics of a Lover, Partner, Sexual Option:

1   Confident

2   Shows Commitment

3   Crazy Fun

4   Very Unpredictable

5   Shows Loyalty

6   Willing to go beyond to prove I am worthy

7   Be very proactive for her

8   Put a smile on her face no matter what

9   Defend her honor

10   Be very challenging

11   Can connect emotionally

12   Brilliant sense of humor

Great list in my opinion. Do you see the subtle difference between friend and lover? Many guys end up in the Friend Zone because they simply don't present themselves as anything other than a friend. Actually what I think a lot of men are doing is attempting to show the woman what a great boyfriend they could potentially be. But ultimately this behavior ends up backfiring, because while they've been on their best future boyfriend behavior, they've also been failing at showing these women the real them.

Guys get so nervous to be in the Friend Zone that they freeze up and forget to put themselves in the sexual, partner zone and ultimately stay in the safe friend zone. They are stuck because they do not know how to change their behavior so that the woman they want will see them as something more.

Trust me when I say I feel the frustration of anyone in the Friend Zone. I have been on both ends of this scenario and neither feel nice. However, wanting someone silently is definitely worse than having your friend want you.

Therefore, I have an assignment for you. I gave the same assignment to this guy. This assignment will help you be clear on how to act with women you want and avoid being stuck in the Friend Zone. A simple assignment will help you decipher the difference between friend and lover.

Assignment:

I want you to write me two lists. One list is a list of the characteristics of a friend. The other is the characteristics of a lover/partner/sexual option. I know in your mind you know the difference, but I want you to be aware of the differences so that you will never present yourself as a friend to a woman you want to do again. This list will help you be clear on how a friend acts vs. how a lover acts.

Do I Stay in the Friend Zone and Wait?
Email:

Hey Marni,

I'm writing to get your advice on an LJBF case I have here. I have known this girl for the last two years. It seems that we're able to spend time together and then eventually we get close and she all of a sudden she seems to freak, puts up a barrier and bust out the "I don't see you that way" line, "let's just be friends" etc.

That has happened a couple of times over the years. Now, in part I realize that it's to do with me not attracting her enough, especially the first time that happened. I am also feeling it has partly to do with her trying to cover up her insecurities too.

We went away together (first time) about a month ago. We had been getting close before that, but no kissing or intimacy of that level. During our trip, we got intimate. We did not sleep together, but she was naked. After which she started crying, and saying how we shouldn't have done that and she doesn't want to lead me on. Since then she has been a bit distant again.

I have been direct with her about it and she said the usual LJBF thing and how she thought I knew that it was just friendship. She said she knows I want more and even said she would only feel comfortable spending time with me if others were there as well. I have heard that line from her before though.

My sticking point is how to approach this. Do I stick to the being friends approach? I have told her to just be my friend now, but that that doesn't mean I don't ever want anything to happen. She knows I care about her.

I have said as much, rightly or wrongly. So would you say I should do the friends thing and just try to build up slowly again? Or, would you suggest going with no contact for at least three or four weeks and trying to re-set things after that?

E

My response:

E,

I guess the first question to ask is, are you okay with just being friends with her for the rest of your life? Meaning there isn't a "wait a year and then..." It's an, "I'm her friend and only her friend and I'm okay with it." If the answer to this is yes, then totally be her friend.

However, if you want something else from her, then the "friendship" is false which is unfair to you and to her. She may have her issues with men but she does not need to work them all out with you, especially if all you get is, lead on, and used for sexual pleasure. Trust me - I have been in her shoes and I know that is what is happening right now. She is not purposely trying to hurt you or lead you on but it is what is happening and you "seem" to be okay with it.

My advice is to think honestly. Are you okay being just friends? If the answer is "no," then it is time to separate from this girl. Give yourself some distance and do not be her faux boyfriend. Date other girls, sleep with other girls, and keep in touch with this girl. I pretty much guarantee there will be a shift in her attraction to you and if not, then you are out dating other girls so she doesn't matter.

Marni

Have I Become "The Friend"? If So, How Do I Escape the Friend Zone?

Email:

Hi Marni,

I am in Mexico and I met a girl at a friend's party last Friday. She came over to where I was chatting with someone and started to use the ashtray. Anyway, it was 11 p.m. and we got talking... and then it was 1 am and we were still talking. At this point, she had to leave, but we exchanged details.

She got in contact with me over the weekend and we met up last night.

From the moment we arrived, I was making her laugh. We shared a food platter and worked our way through crab claws, oysters, lobster - messy hands, bits of shell everywhere; a new experience for both of us (especially the oysters). We were having a great time making such a mess.

However, after a while, we got chatting a bit more deeply, and I think this is where I went a bit wrong. She talked about her son and then her ex (who she had had a row with that very morning because he will not get the message that it is over). She told me the difficulties of their relationship. She then started crying as she talked about the fact that she had gone through so much without having her family around to support - it was obviously very emotional. I comforted her and was understanding.

Should I have done something different here? However, thinking purely of her, I think she found it a real release to be able to talk to me about it all. I find myself caring about her - I am a naturally caring person.

At the end of the night, after going for a walk (during which we messed around, I touched her lots - pushing, poking, flirting, etc.), we ended up at a little bar and chatted some more. It was then getting late, so I walked her to a taxi. This is the bit that I have so little experience of (having only ever actually kissed about five women in my entire life and having been an incredibly shy guy), but I wanted to kiss her.

I went for the kiss and she went straight to the side of my face and said to me, into my ear, "Please don't take this the wrong way, but I'm not in the right place for this right now. It's nothing about you," I told her it was fine and we had a huge hug and she got into the taxi and left.

At one am, she sent me a message to say this: "I'd like to apologize if I seemed overly reserved at the end of the evening, it's hard to explain although I'm sure you probably understand given the conversation earlier in the evening (Sorry - I know I barely shut-up! Next time you get to speak more, promise).

Right now I really am looking to make friends and keep things as simple as possible for the time being, as I really have nothing to offer anyone until I have "repaired" myself a little more and feel more grounded and secure. I hope you're not offended and that you understand."

I told her all was fine and that I totally understood. The frustrating thing is that I know exactly how she feels because I have been in the same place - but I haven't actually had the opportunity to tell her that yet. I told her my heart had ruled my head in that moment, hence, I went for the kiss.

She then replied: "Phew! Was quite worried I had offended you for a moment there. I'm glad you understand because I really enjoyed the time we spent and I'd love to undertake more adventurous ramblings as it was definitely a lot of fun and really made me feel good!"

We are going to meet up again on Friday. Her communication towards me definitely shows interest and, having admitted to me that she hasn't done anything remotely exciting for a long time, we enjoyed and created a memorable experience together.

My question is this: Am I doing things right, or have I just become an agony aunt and a friend?

Thank you Marni,

Alastair

My response:

Alastair,

I don't know this woman but I can get a feeling for where she is at right now. In fact, I am sure that you can understand it better than me because you have been there yourself. To put myself in her shoes, I would think that on vacation, I just want to get away from it all. I would love if some man were able to lead me away from it all. Rather than help me dive further into it.

On this next date, I do not want you to worry about exchanging sob stories with her about your past. I would love for you to touch on it but I would also love for you to let her know that on vacation the rule is to leave your woes behind. Then lead her towards fun. Touch her, look at her with smooth smirks, do the triangle (look from eye to eye then down to lips while she is talking) and keep it light!

This is not going to guarantee it will go to a romantic place but this gives you a better chance of taking it there. If you go in for the kiss again and she gives you the cheek I want you to look her in the eyes and tell her something you appreciate about her and that you would be very mad at yourself if you didn't kiss her.

I know I am always screaming to you guys to listen to women, but this time, stop listening, and start having fun.

Marni

How to Be a Bad Friend but a Freaking Good Lover

Every now and then, you have a good conversation about a very important topic, so I have decided to include the full transcript of my chat with Ryan D about men who are stuck in the Friend Zone and how it can destroy your romantic chances.

To listen to the full audio discussion and download the MP3 go to:

http://www.winggirlmethod.com/Free-Stuff

Enjoy!

Ryan D: Hey everybody, Ryan here, and today I'm very excited because we will be talking about the Friend Zone, how to avoid it and how to get out of it, and to help me, I have my good friend, Marni, from the Wing Girl Method. Marni, how are you doing?

Marni Kinrys: I'm doing very well. I'm glad that you reached out to me about this topic because this is like one of the most pressing issues that I find men deal with every single day. So I love talking about it, and I myself have shoved many men into the Friend Zone over the years so I am the insider who definitely knows how to avoid it and how to get yourself out of it.

Ryan D: Fantastic, fantastic. For me, the Friend Zone is a tragedy. It's men's tragedy because you are in the space that causes desperation.

Marni Kinrys: Exactly.

Ryan D: I believe that there is no man on this planet who deserve that, who deserve to be, desperately wait for a woman to love him. That's why I want to do this product, an apprentice program, Friend Zone Break.

Marni Kinrys: Oh, I completely agree with you with everything that you just said. My belief system actually is that the only person who puts you in the Friend Zone is you. It's not the woman who is actually putting you into the Friend Zone. She's allowing you to be there because she knows for sure that you want her and want to be with her, but because you are not asking to be in any other zone, you are not going to be placed in any other zone because you are not displaying masculine qualities that would elevate you out of the Friend Zone.

Ryan D: So let's get started by what is your definition of the Friend Zone.

Marni Kinrys: Okay, I say I'm not a religious person at all, but I know that many people are, so I relate the Friend Zone to purgatory. Purgatory is a holding space. I think it's a miserable space because it is not definite. You don't know where you are going. You don't know what you are doing. You are always living in fear. You are watching what you say. You are watching what you do because one small little thing that you do could put you into heaven or put you into hell. So it's like the horrible waiting space. It's awful. It's boring and bland. So hell is rejection. Hell is not getting the girl that you want, not being with the girl that you want, not having sex with the girl that you want, but it's definitive. You know exactly if you are not going to, it's rejection.

Ryan D: Yes.

Marni Kinrys: You know you are not getting that girl, which means that you can open up your eyes to a world of what ifs. On the flipside, there is heaven and you do get what you want. You get sex. You get a relationship. You get dating. Whatever it is, those are definitive places, so purgatory is what I relate the Friend Zone to. It's the awful holding space that nobody wants to be in.

Ryan D: Yeah. I agree and I would like to add that the Friend Zone steals your most precious resource that is time.

Marni Kinrys: Yes.

Ryan D: Because you keep waiting. You are in a space where nothing is really happening, okay?

Marni Kinrys: Right.

Ryan D: And it's a tragedy. It's really a tragedy, and there are two aspects to it. On one side, you have to avoid getting into the Friend Zone first, or you can try to get out of the Friend Zone, and that's what we will be talking during this interview.

Marni Kinrys: Yeah.

Ryan D: So Marni, how can a male not know if he is heading to the Friend Zone before it is too late?

Marni Kinrys: Yeah, that's actually a good question. The telltale signs that you are heading to a Friend Zone is when a girl is talking to you about an ex-boyfriend or a current boyfriend. She's calling you at 10 o'clock at night, possibly to cry or to talk and not hang out. Another sign is you go over to her place, you cuddle for an evening, and you do that multiple times in a row. You become her girlfriend. You go shopping with her. She's very comfortable in her pajamas around you. She's comfortable like making a mess of herself around you, and ultimately what it is, it's like that's great. If you want to be friends with the woman and she gets to be that way with you, that's wonderful. However, the telltale sign is when you are in that position and you actually want to be making out with this girl, sleeping with her and dating her.

Ryan D: Yes.

Marni Kinrys: When you are not getting what you want out of the situation, which is the number one sign to you that you are in the Friend Zone. So stop worrying about what she's doing, be more concerned with what you are thinking, feeling, and doing.

Ryan D: Wow! So what can someone do when you first meet a woman to make sure that she doesn't label his as a friend or just to put him in a platonic relationship?

To access FREE bonus materials go to:
http://winggirldatingtips.com/gih-bonuses/

Marni Kinrys: Yeah. I would say the best thing to do is, number one, not allow yourself to become a friend, and when you notice yourself doing friendly things, like she starts talking about her ex-boyfriend, for example, you can put a stop on it and you can say, "We all have baggage absolutely. Let's talk about something more interesting. Tell me about your panties," or something like that. Do you know what I'm saying?

Ryan D: Yeah.

Marni Kinrys: Like pull it back and leave the conversation so that you are not always following her. You are not letting her take the lead. You are not letting her tell you who you are to her and what it is that you can do together. A lot of men that I work with, when they approach a woman, they fire questions at her, and when a woman asks questions back, they are so worried about stating their opinion on something, because they feel like if they say the wrong thing. They could lose her forever that they just become bland and boring and they never state their opinions and they do whatever this girl wants, and that ultimately winds them up in the Friend Zone because they wait for her lead. They wait until she reaches out. They wait until she initiates something. They wait until she invites them somewhere. They wait until she wants to do something. When, in fact, what would get you out of the Friend Zone is doing the exact opposite by telling her what you want and acting accordingly. Not quite being an asshole and not listening and compromising, but by actually taking the lead and saying, "You know what, I want to go to this place." That's great that you want to go there, but let's go there after. But I want to take you to this place and I want to show you why it's so great," rather than, "Sure, I'll do whatever you say."

Ryan D: Got it. Got it. So Marni, do you think that most women make a quick or a rapid decision about men in terms of bad guy friend, bad guy potential boyfriend, bad guy potential lover, or it's more something okay. Can you tell me more about that?

Marni Kinrys: Yeah, well, absolutely. I can tell you that it also changes over time, depending on the actions that the man takes.

Ryan D: Okay.

Marni Kinrys: So I'm going to tell you a story about one woman that I know who is a Penthouse pet actually.

Ryan D: Okay.

Marni Kinrys: So she's a very beautiful woman. She's a model. She is a sex icon for millions of men around the world, so she's wanted basically, and she met this one guy. She flew to LA. She met this one guy. She was there for a week and they just hit it off. They had the best times. She was totally into him having so much, but he never made a move. He never initiated a kiss. He never led her in any way, and by the end of that week, she got frustrated because subconsciously what that woman is thinking is, "I'm not attractive. He doesn't want me. Why won't he man up? I'm not going to approach him and make this happen. Even though I am who I am, I still want to be feminine. I don't want to lunge after some guy and chase after a guy." It's all the things that men think as well. So she got pissed off at him. She was very angered by him at the very end. When women get angry, their tension comes out in a kind of cool way because they don't want to give anything to that guy. They are just like so bitter and they cannot say it aloud like, "Why won't you just kiss me?" Because they don't want to be the aggressor and they don't want to be the man, so at the very end, she basically ended up treating him horribly because she was so angered by him. Then he would still reach out to her all the time in New York and every time that she would get a text or an email, she would say, "What do you want from me? Why are you reaching out to me if you are not going to take action and do something?"

So she went back to New York and he came back to Los Angeles a few months later. They were still in touch and she was so angered and actually felt bad about herself in this situation. She had him pick her up from the airport, not that she took advantage of him, but that's the way that her discomfort and anger were shown where she was like, "I'm going to be around you and I'm going to kind of treat you horribly." It's not meant to be that way at all, but she was just angered and she said to me at the very end, she's like, "Yes, I've had all of this happen. I'm so frustrated and so turned off by him, but if we were driving back to the airport and he pulled the car over the side of the road and said, "Listen, I don't want any of this bullshit anymore. I want you. I want to be with you,' and kissed her." She's like, "I would be with him in two seconds." She's like, "All I want him to do is man up and be the man. I don't want to be the man in this situation. I don't, and I'm frustrated by the fact that he won't take action." I think that that story really shows how easy it is to get into the possible Friend Zone. By taking action, you can get whatever you want, and either you take action and the woman says, "Yuck, I'm not into it," and then you go away and move on to somebody else who is into it, or you take action and you get what you want. But staying in this Friend Zone is just a safe space for both people.

Ryan D: Oh yeah.

Marni Kinrys: The woman gets the guy around her that she knows like he loves her and she gets wonderful admiration and intention, and the guy gets to think that, "One day, we will be together."

Ryan D: Yeah.

Marni Kinrys: That's a wonderful feeling. So it's a safe space for both people, but it actually ends up hurting both people in the end.

Ryan D: So Marni, what you are saying is that many men put themselves into the Friend Zone by not being aggressive enough.

Marni Kinrys: Assertive enough. I don't like the word "aggressive."

Ryan D: Right, yeah, yeah.

Marni Kinrys: But assertive. So there is one other story that I'm going to tell because I want to paint a picture first, and so hopefully people will get lessons out of these stories, so that's the way that I learn best.

Ryan D: Yeah, yeah.

Marni Kinrys: So there was one client that I worked with, and this is like a common thing. So he was out and he met this girl at a bar and they are talking, and within the first four minutes, she mentioned, "Oh my boyfriend." So when a woman says "I have a boyfriend" in conversation, that to her is a silent contract saying to this man, "I have a boyfriend. I'm letting you know that I'm taken, but if you continue talking to me, then you are signing this contract saying you are okay with being friends with me, okay?"

Ryan D: Wow, okay.

Marni Kinrys: So for many guys, on the flipside, they think, "Oh, she's saying she has a boyfriend, but she's trying to challenge me to see if I can push the boyfriend away so I'm going to still pursue her." So do you see how they are both coming at this "friendship" state? They just take friendship from different angles. One is pursuing and getting frustrated if he's not getting what he wants, and the girl is pursuing a friendship with the guy who she thinks or believes understands that she's taken. So again, it's a no-win situation. So the guy that I was working with was getting so frustrated because he would say he would reach out to her to go out and she would go out with him, like go out with a whole group of friends and he didn't understand why she wouldn't want to date him, and so he kept pursuing her. When he said something to her, and she's like, "No, I have a boyfriend. I'm really just interested in being friends with you." And he was so angered and so upset with her because he's like, "Oh, she's leading me on. She's being horrible. She's treating me badly," even though she said in the very beginning, "I'm taken." They signed that silent contract that they are going to be friends.

Ryan D: Yeah.

Marni Kinrys: Even if she's talking bad about her boyfriend that things aren't working, it doesn't mean that you are ultimately going to be the one to be with her.

Ryan D: Yeah.

Marni Kinrys: It means that she is seeing you as a friend and it's the same way that we talked about girlfriends, she's talking about the things that are bothering her and you are her girlfriend to listen, not because she wants you to help her get out of her relationship, okay?

Ryan D: Yeah.

Marni Kinrys: So that's like a different situation of the Friend Zone.

Ryan D: Yeah, yeah.

Marni Kinrys: But it's commonly what I see as well with guys.

Ryan D: Okay, again, do you have seen a woman consciously or subconsciously enjoy the idea to have many male friends?

Marni Kinrys: Absolutely, I loved it when I was younger. I love having guys around me. First of all, I love the guys in general. They are so much easier to hang out with. There wasn't as much pressure. The reason I actually started my company, I think, was that back then I didn't understand how to connect with women. So I learned how to and then how I coach other men how to. I'm married to a man, so I'm not pursuing them for sex or relationships, but it's still the same thing, it's connecting with women and attracting them overall for a long-term basis. So yeah, I love hanging out with guys.

I also loved being around guys that I knew kind of wanted me. I love that my friends some of them at certain times that I know that I could have had my choice if I wanted them. But the truth is, that any of my guy friends, if they actually would have said something to me and they would have said, "I want to be with you," and they rose up on the masculine scale, I would have been with one of them.

But nobody ever said anything, so it was like a nice feeling to be around where I would go up to my friend's cottage and I loved his cottage. I feel so much at home. We were great friends, but we would sleep in the same bed with each other, and it was fun. We would talk all night, and I had loved it. I loved that I love that I had a fake boyfriend, and then I would go fool around with other jackasses or have sex with other jerky guys and hate me and be miserable, and my guy friends will be upset, too, because they weren't with me.

Ryan D: Wow.

Marni Kinrys: Again, I'm going to repeat, if one of them has said to me and/or taken action sexually, I would have done it because I loved every one of them.

Ryan D: Wow!

Marni Kinrys: But they weren't displaying that masculinity that I wanted and needed by taking action.

Ryan D: Yeah, it is very ironic that the guy that you kind of like lost you because he doesn't make a move.

Marni Kinrys: Yeah.

Ryan D: And the guy who is a jerk actually got you because he's confident enough to go after what he wants.

Marni Kinrys: Exactly, and then you get rid them afterwards.

Ryan D: Yeah, yeah.

Marni Kinrys: Because that's what it really, do with you. Actually, I have one girlfriend now who just started dating a guy, and she said that the first time that they hang out; he said something very attractive to her. He said, "I'm going to be honest with you." He's like in his mid-thirties, "So I'm going to be very honest with you, I don't play games.

I'm done with all of that stuff like I'm going to go after what I want. I don't know if I want you yet, but just to let you know, I'm not in this to mess around with your head or mine." And she really appreciated that. She was like, "Oh, that was super sexy that he said that comment."

And since then, for the past two months, he has been quite aggressive with her, but aggressive by calling all the time and contacting and wanting to go on dates, but not very assertive and masculine with her. He's actually quite effeminate. It's kind of turned her off a little bit, but she likes him and she's enjoying him and so recently, she said he did step it up and she is being more assertive and respectful of himself, valuing himself more by taking the lead. And for a while, she was questioning whether she could be with him, even though she really liked him.

So It's sort of like the Friend Zone that I was talking about before. Even though they were being intimate with each other, but she wasn't really enjoying it and she wasn't sure, but she liked him. She wants to keep seeing him to see if there was something there and now that he's being assertive, she's totally into it. She really likes him. He's taking the lead. He's making decisions. He's planning things for them and he's letting her know that he wants to ravage her. He wants to be sexual with her. He doesn't just want to hang out with her and take her to places. She said that was important to her. It's like a big flip in her attraction levels because it makes her want to continue seeing him because she was saying she's a very assertive woman as well.

She's like, "I'm quite assertive, and sometimes people do see me as being more masculine." Even though she's like stunning and beautiful and the least masculine person ever, but she's like, "I need somebody that is more masculine than me. I don't want to be with a girl." She's like, "That's why I'm not a lesbian. So I want to be with a man and a man is somebody who is masculine."

Ryan D: Right. Do you think that there was a point of no return where if a man is not assertive enough and don't make a move, it's lost, and he's going to be put in the Friend Zone?

Marni Kinrys: No, I don't believe that. Women aren't like men, so from my research and my information like I know that men make decisions based on experience, right?

Ryan D: Yeah.

Marni Kinrys: And I feel like women do as well, but women more importantly make decisions based on emotions and feelings.

Ryan D: Yes.

Marni Kinrys: So they can be quickly erased and replaced with new emotions, new feelings, and new memories, but they have to be consistent and congruent. Whatever direction you choose to change with, it has to be consistent and congruent. So for example, even in the Friend Zone for three years, like for my guy friends, we were friends for very long time, and if suddenly, the guy, something switches in him and he says, "Okay, I'm done with the Friend Zone. I don't want to be friends with this girl anymore."

"I realized now I want to be with her and I have to say something." So if one of my guy friends, for example, would have said to me, "You know what? I realized recently I want to be with you. I don't want to be friends with you, and I won't allow myself to be friends with you." So if you said that to me and I said, "Well, I really see you as a friend," which is me saying, "Great, you are making this statement. You are being masculine for this split second." But this is after three years of being in a situation and not two weeks, so three years. So I would think like, "Okay, well, it doesn't really mean anything. You are not really stepping up and being that guy yet."

So in order for that to be effective, so it's what I was saying before about consistent and congruent, that man actually has to step away and say and have the boundary to say, "I will not be your friend." So stepping away from the friendship and not giving me friendship, so he actually has to cut me off in a certain way, or set the boundaries that if he's going to hang out with me, we are going out to date. I cannot sit around my pajamas with him that we are going out at 8 o'clock, we are going for dinner, there is going to be making out at the end, like it has to be pursuing me on a non-friendship level, and that's up to him.

If still I don't want to switch around, then he has to cut me off because it's not healthy for either of us, and ultimately you are not getting what you want. If you want something more from me and I only want a friendship, then that's a relationship that doesn't work, whether it's a friendship relationship or a relationship, we both want separate things.

It's same thing in a marriage. If you want different things and you cannot compromise and work together, then you are not meant to be together. You have to separate and go find what you want.

Ryan D: Yeah.

Marni Kinrys: So again, everything can be switched around as long as the man is consistent and congruent with what he says. If he says he wants more than a friendship, he has to act that way.

Ryan D: Yeah.

Marni Kinrys: He cannot fall back into the friendship again thinking, "Oh well, I said it once so she knows what I want." It doesn't work that way.

Ryan D: I agree with you. I agree with you. So it's very interesting because as you were talking, I realized that the man has many responsibilities in this Friend Zone thing.

Marni Kinrys: Absolutely.

Ryan D: And it's not just, "Oh, that woman put me in the Friend Zone," he kind of put himself in the Friend Zone by not doing what he's supposed to be doing. Does it make...

Marni Kinrys: Absolutely, nobody puts you anywhere. It's the same thing when people say things like, "Oh, they made me feel this way." Nobody made you feel that way. You made yourself that way. The action that they were doing made you feel that way, but you are responsible for your own feelings. Nobody else is responsible to your own feelings. If you keep returning, it's like an abused wife. You keep going back to the guy that's hitting you. Yes, the guy is at fault for hitting, but you are responsible for taking yourself out of your home, and even though it's difficult and challenging, it's your responsibility to remove yourself from that situation, to do everything you can to not be in that situation.

So if a woman says to you, "No, I just want to be friends. I really like you that way. I don't want to ruin our friendship." You say, "Okay, I'm sorry, but I can't be friends with you, and you are going to have to respect me, but I'm going to need to take some space from you for all that. I'll cut it down to maybe an hour a week of hanging out with you or whatever."

Whatever you feel comfortable with in the very beginning, that still establishes yourself as a non-friend, but you can say during that hour, "I'm going to be pursuing you. I'm pursuing you for a relationship, and I'm going to show you that we are meant to be with each other." But if you then go back into the same routine like cuddling and sleeping over at her house and not doing anything or being there and listen to her cry about her boyfriend, then you just said something, but you are not really taking action to following up on your words. So it's kind of like a fake statement.

A woman is not going to take the lead. She will never take a lead. It's the same thing when you approach a woman cold, she is not going to suddenly open up and try to make you comfortable in conversation. In the very beginning if you've approached a woman, it is your job to tell her what you want, either subconsciously or non-verbally.

Ryan D: Oh, wow! I really agree with that. Okay, so let's get to how to turn her into a girlfriend level. We will be talking about it apparently, but let's get more into that. Let's say someone is a friend with a woman for a long time. It was like a year now.

Marni Kinrys: Okay.

Ryan D: How can he change the perception that this woman has of him?

Marni Kinrys: Exactly everything that I just said to you. It's like to change the perception; you have to change the perception of yourself, right?

Ryan D: Yeah.

Marni Kinrys: So I'm not going to see anything unless you show me it. So if you have changed your point of view in the fact that you want to have a relationship now, then I need you to show me that. I need you to step up and be that guy. I am not a mind reader, so I am not going to be able to subconsciously know what you are thinking and feeling, and vice versa, I am concerned with myself.

I'm not concerned with other people. I'm a caring person, and most women are as well, but more importantly, we are concerned about ourselves until we are in a relationship or a friendship or related to somebody where we do grow to care about somebody then you are concerned about other people as well. But yeah, if you need to express these changes, then you have to express the changes and then stick with what you've expressed.

Ryan D: So you are saying that the men should express verbally his intention.

Marni Kinrys: Absolutely.

Ryan D: Or he can you just start to blend where he can non-verbally blend the idea it was more than a friendship.

Marni Kinrys: Well, I guess, the thinking is that I always say if you want something, you have to ask for it.

Ryan D: Okay.

Marni Kinrys: So yes, you can sneakily plant the seed. I don't really know what that would even look like if you secretly planted the seed, like suddenly like grab her boob. I don't know what like the moves that you can make, but I would say, at some point when you are in a calm setting, probably not when you are out of the bar drunk and like fighting, you want to be in a calm space. It's the same thing when you are in a relationship, you don't want to bring things up when other things are going on.

So you say to the girl, "Hey, look, I want to talk to you about something." And if she says okay, and then you say, "Here is what I'm thinking; this is what I've been thinking recently. I realized that we get along really well. I'm very attracted to you and I don't want a friendship with you. I actually want to pursue you. I don't know if we are meant to be in a relationship with one another, but I want to date you. That's what I want." And then she can give her response whatever it is like it can be, "Me, too. I really want to be with you." Or it will be like, "No, I don't want to ruin our friendship."

That's sometimes fear or maybe she's not attracted to you at that point, then okay, and so whatever it is that she says. So if she says, "No, I don't want to that." And then you say to her,

"Okay, that's okay. I do want that. So I'm going to have to take a step back because I have to re-evaluate and think about what I want. But I cannot stay in what we have right now. It's not healthy for me and it's not healthy for you. It's not fair to either of us." So then you take a step back, or you say, "If we are going to hang out, then I'm going to pursue you."

So then when you are pursuing her, then you do sexier things, more dating things. You don't go over to her house at 11 o'clock at night and sitting in your pajamas and like fart in front of her. What you do is at 9 o'clock at night, you say, "All right, we are going for a drink now. Put on a nice dress, and we are going out. I'm taking you out."

And when you are there, you touch her. You don't talk about any ex-boyfriends or about other things. You talk about more fun-like things and you kiss. You are going for the kiss at the end of the night, and if still she doesn't want that and it feels uncomfortable after a couple of weeks, then you say, "Okay, obviously, this isn't something that you want, it's something I want. So we kind of have to break up for a bit."

Ryan D: Is it like pressing the reset button on the friendship, from the relationship?

Marni Kinrys: Absolutely, because you are going in a new direction now. You can still have your friendship there, so you will have that comfort level, but friendship is very different from a relationship.

Ryan D: Yeah.

Marni Kinrys: Like with my husband, I have a friendship with him, but we are in a relationship definitely. We are very comfortable with each other. We share a bathroom, so there are non-sexy things that are involved in our relationship, but we are intimate with each other. We are sexual with each other and sexy around each other, and there are moments of friendship, but if I ever felt that we were in a straight friendship, oh well, that's not a relationship. That's a friendship. So you have to draw that line, and sometimes for people, they have to decide what the difference is for them, like what it looks like.

If you need to make a list, jot down what a relationship means to you. So you can say dating means this, dating means you go out on dates, dating means you make out at the end of the day, dating means you sleep with somebody, so that you have those things in mind as to what dating is and a friendship is.

Ryan D: Right, okay. If a romantic relationship is not possible, do you think that the man should just cut off the relationship?

Marni Kinrys: Absolutely. It doesn't mean you have to be a jerk because you can say to a woman, "Look, this is what I have to do because this is what I want. So can you please respect me and give me some space? I cannot give you the friendship that you want right now, because I have to takecare of myself." And most likely a woman is going to reach out to you and text you most likely when she's drunk because it's a good thing. You were in a relationship of some sorts, so suddenly there is a void in her life. There is a void in your life, too. So just like most relationships where you go back for like break-up sex, it's going to be the same thing with that friendship. She's suddenly are going to reach out to you because you are in her routine, but the thing is that if you make a decision you have to be strong with your decision, and you have to have those boundaries up and you can't help comfort her while you are trying to get over the breakup as well. She has to go and reach out to her other friends and fill that void on her own. It's not your responsibility to help her get through with it.

Ryan D: It's very interesting because I feel subconsciously a lot of men stay in the Friend Zone because they are afraid of what you just said that if you don't want the relationship, you would have to cut off the woman from their life.

Marni Kinrys: Yeah.

Ryan D: And I think it is very tough. It's not easy. What can you tell to the men who are listening who are scared of losing that woman because they will have to make a decision?

Marni Kinrys: Well, you've already lost her basically, and then you lose your manhood if you keep going back to her.

Ryan D: Right.

Marni Kinrys: That's all I have to tell them. That's why it's amazing. It's like you cannot say one thing and then still do another. It's like if you want somebody to believe you and take your word for things and trust what you say, then you can't say, "Okay, I can only be with you if we are in a relationship," and then you start hanging out as friends again, what does that show a woman?

On the flipside, think about it, as someone was to do that to you. If someone says to you, "Yeah, I won't be able to be your gardener anymore." And then comes back every day and gardens for you, what does that mean? It means, "Okay, well, now, you can be my gardener for free. Okay, fine. I'm going to take advantage of that. If you are going to be my gardener, I'll ask you to do certain things." So the thing is that if you are not true to your word, then how can anybody else be?

Ryan D: Yeah, it's true. I agree with that. I really agree with that.

Marni Kinrys: Cool.

Ryan D: So let's go to the other side and when a romantic relationship happened because she likes you and everything is okay. So what can you tell, or what kind of advice and tips can you give to make sure that the relationship works well in the future?

Marni Kinrys: To make sure that the relationship works well in the future. Ooh.

Ryan D: I mean, because they were friends, girlfriend/boyfriend, so it has changed the dynamic of the relationship.

Marni Kinrys: I really believe, and I know everybody says communication is key, but it really is key, communication, and removing your ego from a relationship. A relationship will never succeed if you have your ego inside of that relationship. There is no room for four people in a relationship.

So communication like for me, before I got into a marriage, in a relationship, I really thought communication was just talking to your partner, not like actually talking about things that are uncomfortable and awkward, and shoving your ego aside. So I think that for anybody who is shifting - sorry, I'm changing my chair so maybe I'm making noises - shifting from friendship to a relationship, I think there needs to be a discussion about expectations.

Ryan D: Yeah.

Marni Kinrys: Again, what it looks like, and like having check-ins every once in a while and sit down with each other and just say like, "Okay, what is this new relationship for us look like? Like what do you want in a relationship?" And then vice versa, what do the other person wants, and then check in maybe a month later and say it like, "You know, how is everything going? I'm really enjoying this relationship. I like where it's going. I would like to see more of X, Y, and Z."

Ryan D: Wow!

Marni Kinrys: And then you talk about it in a very safe place. If you already have that friendship and you know each other, it is easier to have those conversations. That takes a while in the beginning of the relationship because most people are afraid to rock the boat by saying what their needs are, what they want, so it gets a little scary. But overall, communication about what you want and need out of a relationship and then hearing the other person's point of view and coming to a compromise or understanding in general is the way that relationship succeed.

It's the same thing with friendships. It's the same thing in family, although family is a whole other different, but with everything, working relationships. You constantly have to express what you are thinking and wanting because you two are not mind readers so they are not going to know to give you something if they don't know that you want it, or they may not even know to do it because they didn't grow up that way. So they don't know that those things are acceptable in your eyes unless you tell them.

Ryan D: Yeah.

Marni Kinrys: So it's constant communication. Sorry, that's a long answer for a short question, but yeah.

Ryan D: Yeah, so making sure that you've gotten all of your expectations.

Marni Kinrys: Exactly.

Ryan D: Okay. Marni, I have one last question for you.

Marni Kinrys: Okay.

Ryan D: Do you believe that men and women can be just friends?

Marni Kinrys: Absolutely, if that's what both people want. I think that there is always that question because if it is a male-female dynamic, you are always thinking, "Hmmm, is this person for me in that way? Should they be? Should he be my boyfriend? Should he be my partner?"

Ryan D: Yeah.

Marni Kinrys: But yeah, I think that male-female friendships can definitely exist. It's just depends like what the other person wants. If both people are honestly and truly really satisfied and happy with the friendship, then absolutely. But if one person wants something more and isn't saying anything, that's not a real friendship. Like I'm home for the holidays right now visiting my friends, and my friends are guys.

I went over to my friend Steve the other day to his house. He bought a house. It's like a block and a half away from my parents, so I went over to his house, and at that time, I could question, "Oh, should I go to Steve? Should I not go to Steve?" I didn't have that obviously. He's married now. I'm married now and it was asexual when we were in there, and it was nice. I'm like, "I like that you can move past that phase and actually be friends." And I know that if I ever did need anything, he would be there. He is my real friend, and vice versa for him.

Ryan D: Oh, wow!

Marni Kinrys: So yes, I do believe that men and women can be friends as long as both sides are honest about what they want.

Ryan D: Wow! And I would like to add that it's always sane to have female friends, just platonic female friends.

Marni Kinrys: Oh yeah. That's the base of my business. If you can have a female friendship that is a real friendship, oh my God, you have like magic at your fingertips. As long as you tell your girlfriends, and I say this to everybody because my company is The Wing Girl Method, you can have your own wing girl at any point in time.

If you tell your girlfriends, "I want the truth from you and I want you to give me real information, even if it hurts my feelings and tell me every-thing that women wants to do and say, don't want." You have to train your women to be honest with you, and it's the same thing in a relation-ship, you can let them know that you can handle what they are going to say because women are going to tell you the truth if you are very clear on the fact that you want it.

Ryan D: Okay. Marni, I already told you that before what I like about you is how you give the real like no BS female perspective. As I said, not the socially accepted female perspective like, "Oh, just be you with this kind of stuff." But really the real stuff, the real stuff.

Marni Kinrys: Oh, thank you. I really appreciate that.

Ryan D: And you are being honest with guys, and that's why you are awesome.

Marni Kinrys: Thank you.

Ryan D: So guys, go to http://www.winggirlmethod.com/ if you want to have Marni as your wing girl and to have all the free stuff, free articles and her newsletter that you get from her website. Marni, thank you very much.

Marni Kinrys: Oh, thank you.

Ryan D: I hope we will have you again for another interview.

Marni Kinrys: Oh, definitely, anytime. I love talking with you. For some reason you give me good energy.

Ryan D: Thank you.

Marni Kinrys: So I always feel like I give valuable information when I talk to you. With other people that I talk to sometimes, I don't deliver the same. I have like a nice connection with you. So anytime that you have a question, ask me.

Ryan D: Thank you. I will for sure. Okay. Talk to you soon. Thank you very much.

Marni Kinrys: Oh.

Ryan D: Talk to you soon, guys. Bye.

Marni Kinrys: Thank you.

She's Just Not That Into You: Don't Mistake Emotional Banter for Flirtatious Banter

Women give guys loads of signs when they're interested in them (in fact you can learn more about these on my Signs She's Into You list) but want to know one sign she's not interested?

When she complains about her boyfriend

Even if she tells you, "I would love to date you if I didn't have a boyfriend" she is not looking for a date, but for an emotional crutch. She does not want to cheat on her boyfriend, or ditch him, in the end; instead, she is just looking for a short-term quick fix of attention.

The woman you like probably is not doing this harmfully, or even fully consciously. All she is aware of is that her boyfriend is not giving her all of the validation, attention, and security that she needs: so she is spreading her wings and seeing if she can plug that gap elsewhere.

She may have just had a fight with him over his boys' night out, be pissed that he hasn't text her back that evening or be feeling insecure after she found out that her guy's ex was a swimwear model. It really could be any number of reasons, small or large, but it is far more about her relationship with him, than her attraction to you.

I know this is not what you want to hear but you may just have just been in the right bar, at the right time, to be on the receiving end of her fishing for attention.

She wants to feel appreciated; however, now, you are not the person she truly wants to feel appreciated by

Therefore, your flirting with her will act like an emotional Band-Aid for now: but as soon as her boyfriend heals the rift, she will not need your attention, dates, or flirtation anymore. She may even feel guilty for having looked to you to fill this emotional void: and will back off completely.

So even if she is:

- Smiling at you

- Touching your arm and leaning in

- Telling you that she thinks you are handsome

If it all comes with her sighing, "I would love to stay in touch if I didn't have a boyfriend," do not take her signs seriously. It's very easy when a girl is giving you these huge signals to ignore the fact that she has a man, and hope that she will cheat on him with you tonight.

While I am not going to pass judgment on any of you guys for thinking that: even if she did cheat, it would create a messy and complicated situation that you would not want to find yourself in! So get out and move on! You can enjoy the flirting in return, but do not get invested. Do not spend hours hanging out with her, listening to her, and pursuing her with endless texts and emails, as this is one clear route straight to the Friend Zone.

So next time you get a girl flirting with you, while telling you she is unavailable, I want you to enjoy the brief flirtation and then move on. Unless you want to be her friend, move on! There will be loads of other women who will want to flirt with you for real. So ditch the emotional banter with taken women, and have flirtatious banter, with single women instead.

To access FREE bonus materials go to:
http://winggirldatingtips.com/gih-bonuses/

What Do I Do If She Starts Talking About Her Guy Problems on a Date?
Email:

Marni,

Here's a question I have not seen the answer to. What do I do about a woman who does nothing but talk to a guy about her problems and depressions? How do I handle this in particular and move things to a more romantic footing (as this is happening to me right now)?

James

My response:

James

Friends let women cry on their shoulders. Men lead them away from their problems. What I am getting at is that it is up to you to shake up the situation that is in front of you. If you go on a date and a woman starts unloading her woes on you, quickly nip that shit in the bud.

There's no crying in baseball and there is certainly no crying on dates. I would never want you to do that on a date.

Women are going to go wherever they are emotionally led to. So if you are on a date and start talking about the "the past" and her "ex," hold her hand for a second and tell her, "We all have a past. We all have been hurt. However, tonight is about tonight. Now, what are you going to get? The sirloin looks good."

Do this, instead of firing off questions at her so that she opens up and tells you more about her abusive ex-husband or past break up that left her in shambles. I know you think that this is polite to do because it shows you can listen, but it is the one-way ticket to friendship town.

So lead away from this conversation. A woman wants a man that can keep her safe and secure. The first step to showing that to her, is that you help her avoid her past by showing her what she could have in the future.

Marni

She Brought Her Ex on Our Date
Email:

Marni,

I went on a date with a girl. It was our second date and she brought along her ex. What does this mean? Is she into me? Confused at what's going on.

Any help would be appreciated.

Max

My response:

Max,

Whoa, Whoa, Whoa! She brought a guy, let alone an ex on your date?

Did you make it clear you were asking her on a date? Did she ask your permission to bring someone along? The answers to these questions do not matter but the message behind them should. If you are not clear with your intentions then a woman is free to interpret how she pleases.

I have to be honest and say she probably knew you wanted to be alone with her but obviously did not want that. If she were into you, she would not have brought along another dude. To me it sounds like this was her subtle way of saying, "I'm not into you, but I am open to being friends."

In the future if this situation happens again, get your self-respect back by saying "I'm asking you on a date and therefore want it to be just the two of us." If she does not feel comfortable with that then she will tell you. Honesty and being clear on what you want are the best time-savers and money-savers in the world.

Remember, you are always allowed to speak your mind as long as you do it from a calm, comfortable place. As soon as you get defensive or accusatory, you lose.

Marni

VI. How Women Want It! The How, What, Where, When and Why Behind Every Female Action.

Eleven Things about Beautiful Women Every Man Must Know

Ah, beautiful women! They are pretty freaking amazing to look at aren't they? Even I look at them.

The other day I was in the car with one of my guy friends, having a great conversation. When suddenly, to our left was a beautiful woman getting into her car: Tall, long legs, short shorts, cowboy boots, curvy hair, and sunglasses. Both of us instantly stopped talking, looked at her, and then continued on our way. It was insane that a beautiful woman would have that much magnetic power over both of us.

It proved to me that everyone loves looking at beautiful women. However, not everyone understands beautiful women. For most, beautiful women are what they see in magazines, or from a social distance. They do not get to

To access FREE bonus materials go to:
http://winggirldatingtips.com/gih-bonuses/

interact with them on a personal level. Today we give you the tools to make things happen. Here are 11 things every man must know about quality, beautiful women:

1   Beautiful Women Don't Have Secret Powers. Yes, they may look great in tight spandex leggings, but contrary to popular belief, beautiful women do not have super powers. The only power they have is their attractiveness, and that can only get a person so far.

2   Beautiful Women Want to Be Approached. I am friends with a super-hot Hollywood actress, (whose name I will not disclose), but trust me she's gorgeous and you know her, and she told me that if she ever wants to be alone, she goes out in public. No one looks at her, no one talks to her, and no one approaches her. The funny thing is she would love to be approached. Most of my girlfriends say exactly the same thing. Their main complaint is that they never are approached. If they do, it's by arrogant, stuck up jerks. So next time you talk yourself out of approaching a beautiful woman, remember, she wants to be approached. You are not bothering her if you are a solid, amazing guy.

3   Beautiful Women Have Insecurities Too! Oh my God, do they have insecurities. Yes, there have been areas in their life that may have been easier because of their looks. However, when it comes down to it, beautiful women have the exact same insecurities running through their head as the rest of the world. Am I good enough? Am I a loser? Am I fat? Is my skin bad? My thighs are horrible. Will they like me? Will they like me for more than my looks?

4   Beautiful Women Are Guarded and Have Baggage. Just like you, they have been hurt, bruised, and wounded from past relationships. I hear many beautiful women say that sometimes people forget that they have feelings and that they are real people. "Some men want to date me so they look better and they don't care about me. I have had this happen to me many times and it hurts. It hurts to be used for your looks" - says my female friend who is a model.

5   Beautiful Women Want a Good Man. Do you know how often normal women are approached by huge D-bags? Well, multiply that by 50, because that's how many approach beautiful women. Why? Because most of the good guys are too afraid to approach. Beautiful women want to be with a good man, not an asshole.

6   Beautiful Women Are Not Necessarily Superficial. Some are, yes. Some aren't. You do not have to have Einstein's brain, George Clooney's looks and Bill Gate's money to attract, date and get a beautiful woman. You have to have all those things if you want to date a superficial money grabber.

7   Beautiful Women Aren't a Bunch of "Stuck Up Bitches." At least not all of them. Like everything else, you come across some good ones and you come across some bad ones. I know it's easier to think all beautiful women, or people for that matter, are stuck up, but they are not.

8   Beautiful Women Have Brains and Want to Have Interesting Conversations. In fact, some of my

To access FREE bonus materials go to:
http://winggirldatingtips.com/gih-bonuses/

most intelligent friends are ridiculously beautiful women. Beautiful women can also have brains and personalities to match their looks — just like all the fives, sixes and sevens of the world.

9   Beautiful Women Don't Want to Be Approached with Compliments on their Looks. Beautiful women do not want to just be beautiful. Like all other women, they want to be heard, seen, and understood. If you want to get a beautiful woman, compliment her on her, rather than the way she looks. She already knows she's hot. Now tell her something she doesn't know.

10   There Is No Right Thing to Say to a Beautiful Woman. I have said this repeatedly, there is no magic panty dropping line that every man can say that will make a woman want him instantly. Line up ten guys in front of me, all saying the exact same pick up line and guaranteed I will feel a different reaction to each of them. Some I will love some I will hate and some will creep me out. It's not about what you say; it's about the man who says it. Character, character, character. Like all other women, beautiful women are just people. Not unicorns with breasts.

11   Do Looks Matter To Women? I wanted to share an interesting yet common story about attracting women. I am sure many times in your life you have been walking down the street, saw a beautiful woman with an unattractive man and said to yourself, "Something is wrong here. Why is she with that guy?" I am sure you could not understand it. It probably frustrated the hell out of you. That is because you were using your male eyes instead of your female eyes to evaluate the situation.

Let me explain.

Unlike men, women are not primarily driven by looks. Looks can be and most often are overridden by personality to a point where a man's features can totally transform in the eyes of a woman. Men make decisions based on facts and women make their decisions based on feelings. Therefore when meeting a new man, women will decide if they are attracted to them because of how that man makes them feel. In man terms, this means looks are not as important to women as they are to men.

When a man first approaches a woman, she judges him entirely on his looks and how he presents himself. What else does she have to judge from? It has only been 5 seconds. However, something interesting happens to a woman when she interacts with others. She starts to feel the other person and from that feeling, she can interpret a person's character and value within a matter of seconds. Their looks start to blur and their appearance changes depending on how they make her feel. I call this energy but it is also known as character.

Regardless of whether you are rich or poor, good looking or plain, fat or thin, bald or hairy, if you can master the art of projecting a quality energy that women can feel, you can light up a woman's primal attraction circuitry like a Christmas tree!

Trust me when I tell you this. All of my girlfriends are with men who are not nearly as attractive as they are. Nor are they rolling in dough. What each of them does have is a strong character that can be sniffed out by women from a mile away.

What Do Women Find Sexy?

I am about to shatter a lot of male fantasies right now by revealing that the things women find sexiest are not at all related to sex. So set aside your hopes of women being turned on by boxer briefs and waxes. In fact, for many women, turn-ons come from simple everyday rituals, mannerisms, and idiosyncrasies. That is because a woman's libido is triggered by her emotions and the way something makes her feel, rather than what it makes her think!

I put out a survey to my circle of female friends, confidants, and Wing Girls (over 200 women). I asked each of them, "What do you find sexy?"

Below are the top 11 responses:

1   **Intelligence without Arrogance:** Intelligence is sexy only when the guy's not attempting to belittle you or be arrogant in the process. It's extremely sexy when a man knows how to maintain his intelligence without riding a high horse in the process.

2   **Voice:** "When I hear a man with a deep voice that comes from his diaphragm it makes my tingle in area's that may not be appropriate to talk about" — DAISY. A deep voice is the ultimate sign of masculinity.

3   **Honesty, Loyalty & Integrity:** Overall these three characteristics speak to a man's character. "The measure of a man's real character is what he would do

if he knew he never would be found out." — Thomas Babington Macaulay. Being an honest, loyal man with integrity will not only turn women on; it will keep them coming back.

4   Good Credit: Probably the most seemingly superficial response from my gaggle of women, but one of the most important. Poor credit can be a huge red flag because it triggers the fear that a man is not reliable, lazy and is not responsible. To save yourself from having your poor rating hold you back from attracting women, it is important to show that you are proactively working on erasing the bad credit and committed to wiping that slate clean.

5   Great Smile: Even though recent studies have found that pictures of men smiling can decrease feelings of attraction from women, my survey proved otherwise. A nice, warm smile from a man can melt a woman's heart and instantly turn her on. "What's important about the smile is not the actual smile itself, but the underlying intention behind the smile. I love it when a man smirks at me in a way that says, I'm thinking something but I'll never tell you"—JEN

6   A True Gentleman: "In all my dating years, I have only had two men open doors for men. One of those men was my first and only one night stand. The other is now my husband" —MONICA

Men! Do not let chivalry die. Open doors, pull out chairs, be polite to everyone. However, do it because you want to, not because you think, it will get you something. That's the true definition of a gentleman.

To access FREE bonus materials go to:
http://winggirldatingtips.com/gih-bonuses/

7 **Taking Out The Garbage Without Being Asked:** "Want to know how to get my panties off in 30 seconds flat. Take out the trash without me having to ask you." —JUSTINE.

Caring gestures make women feel good. Guys do not realize how important they are for women when it comes to being turned on in the bedroom. To connect physically, they really need that emotional and mental connection.

8 **A Sense of Self:** "So many men are like Velcro. They just latch onto you. Especially when they are older or divorced, this is not sexy at all. " —MICA

Have a purpose, have an opinion, have a life, and you will always be the sexiest man in the room.

9 **Sense of Humor:** "If a man can make me laugh, I'm his forever. Sexy, sexy, sexy." —EMILY.

Before you start signing up for comedy classes, I want to be clear about what "I want a guy that makes me laugh" actually means. What a woman is really saying is, I want a guy that is light, fun and does not take himself too seriously. Enjoying life always equals sexy.

10 **Good Communication:** They say communication is the essential foundation to all relationships, but is it sexy? "If I am talking to a man about something and he gets emotional and defensive I am instantly turned off. Seriously. I find it especially sexy if a man can hear me and remain grounded" — ERICHA

11   Confidence: When asked, women often respond that the number one thing they want in a man is confidence! Confidence is nature's signal that "I am not weak." No woman wants to be with a weak man. "A bald man is just as sexy as a man with thick wavy hair if he loves his head." —JENNIE

Confidence tells a woman, "I'm proud of who I am, I respect myself and you will always be safe with me."

You can see the real turns on for women do not include crazy, unachievable sexual fantasies. In fact, what women actually find the sexiest is you being the best you.

Do Women Want Sex As Much As Men Do?

Hell yes! Where did the hideous rumor that women do not like sex start? Of course we do and why wouldn't we? Sex feels good, it is fun, and can release heaps of tension and anxiety. Then why the rumor?

Why this belief that women are not sexual and don't want sex as frequently as men, when there are hundreds of studies that prove they do? When it comes to sexuality, I can tell you as a woman that I feel most liberated when I am in control of the choice to be sexual. Woman don't want to feel used, taken advantage of or empty - as if they could be replaced by anything with breasts for your enjoyment. We want to be part of the experience. We want to be part of the choice to have sex.

We do not want to feel that because we are women we owe someone sex, or that sex has been forced upon us or that we owe sex in exchange for a meal. We want to own the decision, and enjoy every second of the experience.

I'm going to share a story with you.

When I was younger, I was a huge prude. I had tons of guy friends who would take advantage of women and lie to get them in bed. Now, even though these guys never treated me this way, it caused me to put up barriers fearing that all men would do the same thing to me if I let them. I never wanted to be taken advantage of or seen as a slut.

I became the kissing bandit and made a rule to only kiss men until they proved they really liked me and would never use me. I made men jump through hoops to get any more from me. That was until I went backpacking and met a man who changed it all for me. A man that got me to open up in just one night.

I was out with my girlfriends one night in a little town called Byron Bay that was filled with tons of other backpackers from around the world. We got to one bar that we loved and planted ourselves in our usual spot when I suddenly spotted this cute blonde guy across the bar.

Now this guy was not attractive because of his looks. In fact, this guy was five foot five, super skinny, and not my type at all. I found him attractive because of the way that he was acting. I could tell right away he was the leader of his group and he was ensuring his whole group was having a great time. He didn't focus on girls; in fact, he didn't seem concerned with anyone other than his friends. He was focused on having fun and getting the most out of his evening.

I immediately thought, "I want him." I grabbed my girlfriend and made her come with me so that we could stand near the group and catch his attention. Five minutes later and nothing had happened. I was pissed and felt unattractive. Then suddenly he walked by us, said something, which I cannot even remember, and went back to enjoying his friends. I was extremely turned on.

Towards the end of the night, as we were ready to leave, he approached me and we started talking. He offered to walk me back to my hostel, which he happened to be staying at as well and I of course said yes. We got back to my place, I invited him in, and we instantly started kissing and moved our way to my bed. Then as soon as he tried to go further than kissing, I immediately tensed up and got scared.

That is when he did the best thing any guy had ever done with me. He stopped, looked at me, and said, "If you are uncomfortable with anything we're doing I want you to slap my hand and we'll stop immediately." He literally took my hand and slapped his own.

Just hearing those words immediately calmed me down and got me to open up liked I have never done before. That was my first ever one night stand. So what is it about those words that got me to throw away all my boundaries? It occurred to me that this guy understood women--something that I had never encountered before. With just a few simple words and a little eye contact, this guy was able to communicate four things to me:

1   I was in control of my sexuality.

2   I could choose what I wanted.

3   He wasn't going to force me to do anything I didn't want to do.

4   Most importantly, he was okay with whatever I chose.

       This immediately took away the pressure and allowed me to do something I had never done before: be in control of my own sexuality. It was amazing!

Choosing to be sexual can be empowering and liberating. So learn from this advice above and stay calm, cool, and collected. You will start to see women reacting differently to you both in the bedroom and in the rest of the world.

Ten Ways to Get Her in the Mood

       I am about to rock your world by revealing the #1 myth about women and sex. Ready for it? Women want sex just as much, if not more than men do. Women are sexual, sensual beasts waiting to be released by the right man in just the right way.

       Here are Ten Ways to Get Her in the Mood whether you are dating, simply seducing, or in a long-term relationship.

       1   **Get Her Out of Her Head**. The number one thing that blocks or stops women from enjoying a sexual or sensual experience is that thing on top of her shoulders. Her head. For women, sex is far more mental than physical. The more you help make women feel accepted, attractive and safe during any sexual act, the freer she will be. When you provide a safe space it allows a woman's mind to free itself of

insecurities and actually enjoy being in the moment. If you ease her mind, you will loosen her body!

2   **Calm Her Nerves**. My nickname in high school was The Kissing Bandit, which was a fancy way of calling me a prude. When I was 18, I went backpacking in Australia and safely kissed my way up the east coast. That is, until I met a guy who broke me out of my shell. I met him at a club, we went back to our hostel and started making out. Prude Marni kicked in. I clenched and got uncomfortable. He noticed my quick change in behavior and said to me "I want you to be comfortable. If I do anything that makes you nervous or uncomfortable, just slap my hand and I will stop immediately." I can tell you there was no hand slapping that night and I quickly got rid of my childhood nickname.

3   **Tell Her Exactly What You Want**. It drives me wild when a man tells me exactly what he wants to do to me. It's exciting and sexy. Be a man, say exactly what they want, and you will get to beat around the bush, but in a very different way!

4   **Pay Her a Real Compliment, Not an Exaggerated One**. Give a woman a real compliment about her inner core rather than her exterior. Evolutionary psychologists show that women are programmed to be skeptical of what men say. It's their way of protecting themselves from manipulative men who do not want to commit to relationships. The more a compliment is tailored to that specific woman, the

To access FREE bonus materials go to:
http://winggirldatingtips.com/gih-bonuses/

more intimate and effective it is, says Tammy Nelson Ph.D (Kinrys, 2012).

5   **Treat Her like A Lady**. Whether it's for a one-night stand or for a partner of six years, no woman wants to feel like she's a slut, a whore or a stupid female that's been used. Make sure to treat every woman with respect. Be honest, do not manipulate, and treat her like a lady.

6   **Whip Out Your...Intelligence**. Now this may just be me but I get a "hard on" for men who are intelligent. Not the arrogant ones who want to attempt to school me on how much they know. The ones that just seem to know about stuff and talk about it with confidence and authority.

7   **Tease Her in Public**. I'm not talking about pulling her hair and telling her she smells. I'm talking about being covertly inappropriate while out in public. For example, while sitting across the table from friends, talking about politics, slide your fingers up her thigh and just around her underwear line. Do this for about 15 seconds and then remove your hand. Do a couple of these in a night and she will attack you as soon as you walk in the door.

8   **Bring Out Your Inner Caveman**. Nothing puts me in the mood faster than when I can feel my man craving me. "Women love to feel the desire of a man they're into. Give your girl an unexpected, passionate kiss. Grab her hair - gently - and run your hands through it as your lips lock. Moreover, when dinner's over, pick her up over your shoulder, carry her into the

bedroom, and toss her onto the bed. A little spank won't hurt along the way." - Christian Hudson, the Social Man.

9 **Start Flirting At 9am**. Anticipation is one of the most amazing aphrodisiacs. Send her 3-4 texts throughout the day telling her what you are going to do to her in the evening. Tell her how hot she is, that she turns you on and then tell her you like it when she does X. X is the thing that is unique to just her so that she knows your lines aren't canned. One Note: Do not get offended if she does not respond right away or even at all. Many women are not comfortable with this type of forwardness because they do not know how to respond. Just keep going. This shows her you are comfortable being sexual and she can be too!

10 **Touch Her Slowly!** I just got shivers writing this one. Nothing turns me on more than when a man slowly touches me all over my body. Starting with a light massage of my feet. Then working up the leg to the inner portion of my thighs. Moving onto caressing the sides of my belly and chest and ending by brushing my back and neck with his lips. Amazing!

Eight Signs That She Is Flirting with You

Want to know eight easy ways to spot if a woman is flirting with you? Now, I do not believe in waiting for signs before you take action. When you consider approaching a woman the only thing you need to think is, "I am interested in her and want to know more." Once you get into a conversation with a woman, it can be difficult to spot her flirting signs.

To access FREE bonus materials go to:
http://winggirldatingtips.com/gih-bonuses/

First, here are some signs she is not interested:

- No eye contact

- Body shifted away from you

- Arms crossed

- Leaning back

- Looking around the room while you are talking (instead of looking at you.)

- Nodding instead of responding

- Giving one word responses

- Being overly friendly

If you see these signs, run. Get away and get over this woman. She is not into you. Now on to signs you should be looking for.

1   **The Smile**. Remember; do not wait for a smile. You like her, you approach her, and then you decide. If you have a situation where the woman says "whoops thought you were someone else" let her know it was okay for her to make that mistake but you are still sticking around cause you want to know more about her "whoops, I think your hot and could have a good personality that I may like. Let's see if you do."

2   **The Hair**. This is something that I do when I am into a guy and want him to be attracted to me. I twirl my hair, touch my lips, and bat my eyes. All very

feminine flirty things that, as women, we feel will turn a man on and make him more attracted to us.

3   **Change in Appearance**. It is definitely a sign when she returns from the bathroom with new lip-gloss applied, her hair tossed, and a one less button done up.

4   **Asking for Help**. I, like many women have asked for help when it was not needed just to catch someone's attention. "Can you help me lift this heavy chair for me?" I do yoga and weight training and could totally lift it myself but why do it yourself when there is a cute guy that could do it for you?

5   **Body Language**. When I am attracted to someone, I stumble over my words and fidget. We all get nervous. Look for where those feet are pointing.

6   **Conversation**. I have done this myself when I am attracted to a guy. I will be fascinated by anything that comes out of his mouth. Remember, if a woman is not interested she will give you single-word answers and nod. If you have a woman engaged but you can tell she is slightly nervous, it is a sign she is into you.

7   **Openness**. This is a tricky one because most women who are that comfortable with you right off the bat are usually not attracted to you. Therefore, they may freely reveal lots of private information with little worry because there is no attraction to be lost. Make sure that the woman is showing you at least three other flirting signs before viewing this as a positive indicator.

To access FREE bonus materials go to:
http://winggirldatingtips.com/gih-bonuses/

8   **Showing Off**. This is a huge sign that you have created attraction. When a woman starts to validate herself to you, slipping in facts about why she's great, it's a sure fire sign that you have ignited the fire within! You have her bubbling and it is showing through her nerves and desire for you to pay attention to her.

This is probably the most important sign of all that lets you know a woman is totally into you. When in the "approach" phase, if a woman starts bragging about something off topic from what you are discussing, she is attempting to show value. She is attracted.

The Three Magic Words Every Woman Wants To Hear

Want to know the three most important words you can say to a woman that will keep her wanting you forever? "I appreciate you." Seriously. These three magic words are what every woman wants to hear, whether you're talking to her for the first time, on your third date, getting your sexy time on or are deep in a relationship.

Why? Because being appreciated makes a woman, feel seen, heard, and understood. I will break it down a little further for you. When you tell a woman you appreciate her, especially for a quality other than her looks, here's what she hears, "I see something special in you even if you don't see it in yourself." Verbal gold! Just writing those made me tingle.

Believe it or not, when you genuinely express to a woman that there is something special about her, she will slowly become addicted to you. She will do anything to be around you so she can experience that feeling repeatedly and over again. I wanted to paint you a clear picture of the many different ways you can express the three magic words to a woman. I reached out to my network of beautiful, sexy, amazing women and asked them to give me their best examples.

Here are ten ways to express these three magic words to a woman and keep her coming back for more.

1   "I met at a guy at Starbucks last week who told me I had the most unique way of ordering my coffee. He said it with a little smirk and warm eyes and lightly grazed my upper arm. I honestly got chills. Good chills." —BRENDA, 32

2   "I love it when my boyfriend tells me I do something better than his ex. I know it's childish but I love it. It makes me want to continue doing those things and happy to be with him." —JUSTINE, 27

3   "I screwed up and asked my man the 'do I look fat' question. He responded by looking me up and down with a devious grin on his face, threw me on the bed, and told me he wanted to ravage me. Best sex we've ever had." —JENN, 28

4   "Gentlemen are honestly, a dying breed. The men that keep me coming back for more are the ones, who open car doors, have something to say and listen to me when I talk. These men are rare. So when you find one, keep him." — MELANIE, 31

To access FREE bonus materials go to:
http://winggirldatingtips.com/gih-bonuses/

5   "I think because I am so assertive or "masculine" in my day to day life, I really like to feel feminine and lead in my relationships with men. Men who appreciate that about me are men I will continue to be with." —DANIELLE, 28

6   "My husband appreciates me for the stupid little things that I do like putting his clothes in the dryer. I believe it's what keeps our marriage strong and healthy." —SHERRY, 43

7   "Just because you are in a relationship does not mean you stop flirting. My boyfriend walks into our home about twice a week, slaps my ass and tells me how freaking sexy I am and that he cannot wait to get me in the bedroom. Now that definitely keeps me coming back for more." —KELLY, 28

8   "I can tell when a guy is approaching me with his penis. I feel it instantly. A guy who's present and can stay in the conversation with me is a guy whose phone call I'll be answering the next day." —HEATHER, 26

9   "The men that take the time to connect to my mind first, then my body, are the men that get to see my wild side the bedroom. If they aren't in it with me, I close up all over." —STACY, 33

10   "The best thing any man has ever said to me was - I don't know what's going on, but I want you to know I care about you even when you're at your worst. Just know I'm not going anywhere." — JORDYN, 36

Being appreciative of a woman for who she is may not seem glamorous or sexy. I guarantee it is the quickest way to impress her and keep her coming back for more. Communication is so important in a relationship - heck, it's important in every aspect of life and if you learn how to communicate with her just right, you can be her hero without even trying.

How to Be Her Hero

"Nothing" is the worst word a man can possibly hear coming out of a woman's mouth.

"What's wrong?" "Nothing." Gives you shivers, doesn't it.

It doesn't have to be the bane of your existence. I want to tell you what this nothing really means, why we say it, and how it has nothing to do with you. If you can learn how to handle the "nothing" with class, comfort, and ease, you will be a woman's hero for life! I will explain it by using an email that I received.

Email from E:

Hey Marni,

I'm curious about something. When you can see that something is on a woman's mind or is troubling her, when you ask her, "Is something wrong?" or "What's on your mind?" females usually say, "It's nothing." However, my gut feeling is that nothing is something she does not want to tell you. If I am right Marni, what is the best way to handle that situation? Should I just let it go? What's really happening here?

To access FREE bonus materials go to:
http://winggirldatingtips.com/gih-bonuses/

My response:

E,

Ah, the dreaded nothing statement I have made oh so many times. This nothing is actually quite loaded, but not in the way you think. I have heard many men label this as a test or a way for women to manipulate.

It is neither. What it actually is a statement stemming from discomfort.

Nothing means either, "You should know and I can't believe you don't," or, "I am mad at myself for being this mad about X and need your help calming down. I don't want to be this upset, but I am." Both come from a place of caring about you, feeling alone, and discomfort. Both should be handled in the same way.

Let me back up for a minute and tell you something about women. Women tend to think they are in control at all times. They also aim to be an ideal woman, especially in the eyes of the man they are seeing. When they get into situations where they begin to feel "less than ideal," it creates anxiety - anxiety that is uncontrollable and so uncomfortable.

When she is seemingly sitting and stewing, this is the moment where you can be a woman's hero or you can be her punching bag. Ultimately, this choice is up to you because it is really in your control, not hers. If you wish to be the punching bag, engage her defensively, and tell her that, what she is feeling is irrational/crazy/unacceptable. No good. Gets you nowhere but the doghouse for a full week.

If you wish to be a woman's hero stay strong, listen, be patient, and understand that it's not about you. Next, you engage her in a warm way. Not defensive, not attacking and not afraid. The last one is most important. If you show any indication that, you are afraid or that for one minute you are thinking in your head, "this chick's crazy" game over.

You say to her, "I can tell something is bothering you and I want to talk about it with you." Then you listen to her. If she still does not budge, you say, "Listen, I want you to be comfortable telling me things. If I have done something to upset you, I want to know what, so that I can try to not do it again." Give her a hug if needed.

If she still sticks with the huffing and puffing, that is when you have to have a boundary and you say to her, "I can tell something is wrong but I am not going to push it out of you. I will be in the other room and when you are ready to talk, and I will be ready to listen to you." Then leave.

Most likely, she will calm down and eventually work up the courage to speak with you. Still be strong, patient, and understanding and listen to what she is saying. These are her feelings; they are not meant to hurt you or attack you. They are meant to show you what she is feeling so that you can grow together.

Sometimes in relationships, your partner can make mistakes or they can have a moment of weakness. These are the most important times to show her you still care and can handle her imperfections. If you handle these situations with class and calmness, these situations will happen fewer and farther between and you truly will be a woman's hero. Trust me!

Marni

To access FREE bonus materials go to:
http://winggirldatingtips.com/gih-bonuses/

Situations like the one described above can either hurt a couple or bring them closer together. Next time you encounter the nothing situation with the girl you are dating, take it as a compliment. Seriously. Understand that she cares about you enough to feel stress, anxiety, and discomfort over you. If she did not care about you and if she was not invested, then these things would not matter to her.

How to Win Over a Bitch

Want to know how to win over a bitch? From the pretty girl that punched you on the playground in first grade to the model type that gave you a blank stare when you tried to buy her a drink last Friday, I bet you have encountered a pretty girl who just happens to be a total bitch.

At least you think she is, and you have no idea how to handle her tantrums, mean remarks, and cold silences. She only seems capable of being nice to her girlfriends or real players; and you have no idea how to show her you are a decent guy, who deserves a lead role in her life.

Frustrating, huh?

Well I know you might not believe me when I say this, so bear with me, but sometimes it's not that easy being super-hot. You may think that it is all queue jumping, free drinks, and apparently a license to be mean to strangers; but if you speak to hot girls, they will paint you a much less glamorous picture.

I'm good friends with many seriously hot women (I am talking Victoria's Secret hot) and they always complain to me about being judged in the same way. They tell me about how people often assume they are dumb, bitchy, or easy. Each of them will have a story to tell about a guy that only dated them for how they looked, their opinions not being taken seriously at work, and another woman being a real bitch to them, all because of how they look.

You can guess their reaction to always being isolated because of how they look, developing a shield of guarded, thorny behavior that will sting you if you get too close. In keeping you at arm's length, they are not trying to attack you though they are defending themselves. Okay, I know what you are thinking as you read, "Well that's stupid, as that bitchy behavior is keeping me away. I'm a really, genuine guy who would never mistreat a girl."

Yes, you are right; the only guys that tend to break through a bitch woman's defenses are usually exactly the kind of guy that she would want to keep away, the total idiots. It would be great if these gorgeous girls realized that bitchiness is not a brilliant way to meet cool guys: but this is just how things are.

I know it's not very logical, but this behavior is often an unconscious choice It's just a knee jerk reaction. Snapping at you to get out of their way is often no more of a well thought out response than when you were caught sneaking out of school, and just said the first words that came flying out of your mouth.

Knowing why a hot girl sometimes acts like a bitch though will help you figure out how to break down that barrier. You won't be able to sooth it by being the ultimate Mr. Nice guy, because if you pander to her bad behavior by doing whatever she wants, she's not going to respect you.

To access FREE bonus materials go to:
http://winggirldatingtips.com/gih-bonuses/

Moreover, these girls need a strong man they can trust to protect them, so that they do not have to do the hard work themselves.

I want you to show her that you are not fazed by her bitchiness and that you can see beyond their tough exterior shell. Next time you get a bitchy response from a woman let it wash over you; do not react in an overly emotional way. Instead, try to see her behavior for what it really is a defense. Be super cool, ignore her low blow.

A great technique to do this? Start interpreting her bitchy swipes as charming and endearing: instead of cruel and evil. Realize they are not really aimed at you, and fall for the girl that wants to be cared for, not the great pair of legs she comes with. Remember, I am not here to tell you how women should do things. I'm here to tell you how they do things so that you can be ready to win every time!

Why Do Women Flake on Plans?

Have you ever made plans with a women and then 30 minutes before meeting she sends you a text saying "Totally forgot I have plans to meet my grandmother and can't make it." Or, "Seems work has called me in last minute. Can we reschedule?" I can tell you that this woman did not just remember she had plans. She is flaking. She is a female flake.

When a woman likes a man, there is no way she would cancel plans on him for something else. If she does cancel, she will make certain they have concrete plans in the future.

How do I know?

I know because I have done this to men several times. So have each of my Wing Girls and so have each of my female friends. So the question is why do women do this? Unbeknownst to them, women do this because they are selfish. To avoid their own discomfort they will be polite and accept an invite with absolutely no plans of ever following through.

I do want to add that this is not intended to be malicious behavior. It is in no way planned or meant to be cruel. Women are not trying to embarrass you. It is simply done to avoid an awkward situation. It is easier to say yes to an invite or give out a phone number than to say no. At least that is what most women feel and what I felt in the past. They would much rather avoid the phone or flake on a date rather than being rude and saying no to your face. Again, this is selfish behavior based in female insecurity.

Women do not realize how hurtful these actions are to another person. They do not realize the frustration, annoyance and hurt men experience when a woman flakes on them. They think they have avoided being mean and rude when in fact their actions were actually crueler. I cannot teach the women of the world why this is so painful to the men they hurt, but I can provide you with tips on how to protect yourself against the flakes! These tips will help you ensure you do not waste time, money, and energy on women that are not into you.

Tip One - Don't Get Angry

When a woman texts you 15 minutes before your date that she forgot she has another obligation, understand that this means she is not into you. Instead of being angry or hurt about her flaking, feel sorry for her because she was not mature enough to be honest. This will create a calmness in you because you will realize that this is the type of woman that is not worthy of being with you. A woman who cannot speak the truth is not worthy of your attention nor is she mature enough to handle you.

If you like, you can express your disappointment in a mature manner that lets her know you will not accept this behavior. Again, do not be a dick, but maturely express that flaking is not cool. For example, write something like, "Totally understand that things can slip the mind. In the future, it would be best to check your schedule so that you are aware of your commitments. My time is very valuable to me and I hope you will respect that in the future. No hard feelings. Have fun at your event!"

Its firm shows you have respect for yourself and is soft at the end to let her know you are still safe. I hope that she will learn that her behavior was not cool and either correct it with you or correct it in the future. Either way a good deed has come out of the situation.

Tip Two - Do Not Leave the House Before Confirming

To save yourself a drive text her before you leave your home about an hour before you are set to meet. Say, "Running about 10 minutes late. Hope that is still cool?" This text gives her the time to take her out if she wants it. Truth is if a woman is going to flake she is going to flake, but at least with this move you can save yourself time, money, and energy.

Tip Three - Learn to Spot Signs of Interest

The possible flake date can be avoided by knowing what it looks like when a woman is interested in you. I must add that these are not foolproof signs to look for because circumstance can play a role in many interactions. She may be on the rocks with an ex, she may be super stressed in her own life, she may be getting over a break up, she may have just been up for flirting that evening. There are many reasons why she is very hot for you one night and not the next.

Another example is meeting someone else. Attractive, quality women may meet someone else that they are more interested in. Therefore, they will now put their energy into this new guy.

To make sure you are on the right track look for these signs that she is interested in you:

- Making eye contact.

- Ignoring her friends even if it is a Girls' Night.

- Slightly touching you (too much means Friend Zone danger.)

- Engagement in conversation.

- Twirling her hair.

- Puckering her lips.

- Going to the bathroom to get all touched up and looking fresh.

Once you ask for her phone number, listen for the pause. The awkward pause where she debates whether to give you a real number or a fake number. Most women who want you to call have been waiting for this question to come out of your mouth. Meaning there should be no pause.

To access FREE bonus materials go to:
http://winggirldatingtips.com/gih-bonuses/

A pause usually translates into possible flake. These tips will assist you in determining whether a woman flakes on you and will assist you in dealing with a flake. The important thing to remember is that when a woman is a flake, it is a reflection of her as a person, not you. It shows that she is not confident enough in herself to give a real honest answer and is scared to look bad in someone's eyes.

I have learned my lesson about flaking and try to teach every woman I encounter the importance of being upfront and honest. Again, I will do my part to stop this from happening and you should do your part to stop it from happening to you!

Why Do Women "Test" Men: The Shit Test Explained

Doesn't sound like something you want to deal with when you're just trying to take a girl out on a date, or when you've just got home from work, does it? This is why so many times when men are hit with the shit test, they react negatively to what they see as a woman using catty remarks to keep a scorecard on them. Nevertheless, what if I was to tell you that the shit test is really just a strong indicator of a woman's feelings of vulnerability about herself and her attraction towards you?

The problem is that most guys fail to realize that when a woman is slinging all these challenges at them she is not trying to be a bitch, and that they are not being a chump for putting up with it. Yes, it can be a way of sorting out the men from the pussies and testing that you are a guy worthy of her. Yes, it can be a way of her saying, "I'm Queen, and I have the power to choose." However, that's only half the story.

Another important thing to consider is that shit tests often demonstrates a woman's attraction for you and the fact that she feels vulnerable about that attraction. A woman will use a shit test as a way of seeing if you are a man that will stand by her and accept her, warts and all. While you see her as the prettiest, smartest, girl at the party, she'll be testing you with road blocks like:

- "I'm thirsty: I can't talk with a man until he buys me a drink"
- "I wish I was hot/ young/ slim/ pretty like that waitress. She's beautiful, don't you think?"
- "You're far too charming. I think you must be quite the player."
- "Do you want me to tell that joke again more slowly? You're a little slow, aren't you?"

A lot of the time, these mean remarks serve to hide her insecurities about whether you'll stick around when she's got no make-up on and has morning breath. Sometimes consciously, sometimes subconsciously, she is testing your attraction and commitment to her. She wants to know that you will still adore her, above all the other girls, when you hit the inevitable trials a relationship brings up later.

Most Pick-Up Artists would tell you to change the subject if she shit tests you. That is great if you are only interested in a fast route into her pants (which you are not guaranteed to get), but real, long-lasting attraction is about taking the strong, masculine position and reassuring her, "It's ok, calm down, you're amazing just as you are."

Keep your tone of voice confident. This is not being weak. This is being strong and smart. You need to understand that she is not angry with you when she snaps at you for not remembering the shopping, or glares at you for catching the server's eye. The shit tests that come later on in the dating stage are an expression of her insecurities. Realize that this moment is about her, not you. A lot of the time, she may not realize her needs are there until they creep up on her in a moment of insecurity.

She might need to be loved, to have passion in her life, to have someone send a simple text message to say good night. What may seem like a minor offense to you, like sneaking a peak at a passing server's butt, can become a major crime if the woman you are with already feels insecure about herself or her relationship with you. While the initial moment of that shit test is the worst, it does not necessarily get better. It can continue to worsen and you probably cannot help but wonder why she is still mad. You are frustrated and she is still upset, and will continue to be upset as long as she thinks about you witnessing her vulnerability.

Do not try to rationalize everything. Do not try to fix things. Just be there for her. Be masculine and show her the strength she needs for stability. Defensiveness, apologies, or arguments only worsen the situation.

Even the shit test lines you get early on can often be handled the same way:

- By not reacting negatively, but by being sure enough of yourself, that you can provide support to her.

- By having that strength of masculine presence to resist the challenges she throws at you.

- By seeing her snide remarks as a way of inciting sexual tension and desire in a man she is considering as a partner.

- By being James Bond cool, collected, and confident enough to turn her negative emotions into positive examples of your masculinity.

Here are some great examples of how you could turn around the shit tests I discussed earlier and demonstrate how attractive you are as a man:

Example One: "I'm thirsty: I can't talk with a man until he buys me a drink."

"I was about to get you a drink, but I didn't want you to think I wanted to get you drunk. I quite like you just like this, actually."

Example Two: "I wish I was hot/ young/ slim/ pretty like that waitress. She's beautiful, don't you think?"

"The waitress is okay (then look at your date with desire), but you're the hottest girl here (watch her blush.)"

Example Three: "You're far too charming. I think you must be quite the player."

"Of course I'm a player, just looking for the right woman to reform me (wink)."

Example Four: "Do you want me to tell that joke again more slowly? You're a little slow, aren't you?"

"I guess I'll just have to prove you wrong about how smart I am though when we have our first date next week."

Just remember, if you can maintain the strong, masculine position in her life while she has a full-blown melt down, it will not only stabilize your bond with her but also create more attraction. Recognize that shit tests often come from her vulnerabilities, and not your mistakes. Sail over these obstacles and she will find you even sexier.

How to Pass Shit Tests
Here's a question from another client:

In the blog post on your site about shit tests, there are comments saying that women test men to "get what they're due," and to try and weed out someone "worthy" right away.

It also seems like there is very little sympathy at all for any guys who struggle with a test, at any point in the interaction. It is like, oh sorry, I'm not perfect either, I'm not going to come up with a suave answer that solves all your insecurities on cue, every time you have one come up.

These are some questions I seriously could use some assistance in dealing with, and would love help understanding and getting over, especially from a knowledgeable person like you. I don't like having these negative thoughts, and I feel they hold back my development.

Thanks for reading, Marni, Dustin

My response:

Dustin,

When it comes to shit tests, my stance is that men should stop thinking of these actions from women as tests or manipulation. When women test a man, what they are really doing is covering up anxiety, insecurity, or discomfort. It is never a good woman's goal to hurt a man or put him through the ringer. What she is doing is protecting her first. This may come across as confusing and contradictory to men, but again it's for protection.

So what do you do in this situation? You stay strong and grounded. My comments were not to tell men to simply man up and take what they get. The message was for men to understand that women are just as nervous and scared as you are. The sooner you can understand that about women, the better!

Marni

Is She A Gold Digger?
Email:

Hey Marni

Let me ask you a question.

You have a relationship with a man. Essentially, it is a reciprocal relationship. The guy comes into a situation where he is able to negotiate a scenario where his salary is doubled. He was doing well already. Now he is doing, well, obscenely well.

Do you think it is wrong for said man to feel insulted if, on mention of this advancement, that said woman starts discussing marriage? Topic never mentioned before? I personally feel this is a break up situation, but I would love a woman's perspective!

To access FREE bonus materials go to:
http://winggirldatingtips.com/gih-bonuses/

Josh

My response:

Josh

Not at all and for numerous reasons. Do you think this is a gold digging scenario? I obviously do not know full details of the story or the two parties involved but I do not think this is gold digger scenario. I actually think it is a very typical scenario that men and women experience.

I know that with my husband, his earnings were a big part of why we were not married. Or why we delayed marriage for five years. Not because I wanted him to earn more but because he wanted to earn more for himself before we got married.

You may or may not know this, but men are single-focused. This means they focus on one goal at a time and when the goal is complete, they are ready to battle the next goal. For my husband, his first goal was financial and career stability. He felt that once he obtained this goal then he would be "ready" to have support, love, and a family. I was part of this second goal and after many conversations, I knew that.

For this woman, she may have been waiting for him to be more settled and now that he is, she wants to go to the next stage as well.

Let me ask you a question: How is it ever bad when a woman wants to marry you? When she wants to give everything to you? Sounds good to me! That means she thinks you are a great mate for life. Having every-thing balanced just makes her more confident in her choice for a partner.

It's not always black and white, Josh. If these gold digger qualities have never appeared before, then most likely she is not a gold digger. You have to also evaluate character and really try to understand where someone is coming from before jumping to conclusions. That is why communication, real communication, is so important. I must add that your conclusions were defensive, protective conclusions. Be careful of those as they can get you into trouble.

My advice is to have a conversation with your woman about these fears. Be sure to be calm and open, instead of protective and defensive. Give the woman a chance to explain her way of thinking.

Marni

How Do I Breakup with A Girl and Still Be Friends?
Email:

Hey Marni,

I have been through your materials and newsletters, which have been impressive, and it would be a great idea to get to know woman's perspective on this.

There are many personalities out there teaching how to get girls but hardly anyone who mentions anything regarding how to break up with a girl without causing any heartbreak. It feels great to be in control of your love life; that is what we are taught but I find myself clueless when the situation demands a breakup. Say, for instance, I am moving away to a new place and not really in favor of a long distance relationship.

To access FREE bonus materials go to:
http://winggirldatingtips.com/gih-bonuses/

My question is how do I break up with a girl and still be great friends, following which I can move into a new relationship with happy memories of previous one?

Raj

My response:

Raj

Great question.

The first thing I want to tell you is that no matter how hard you try to be good in a break up, becoming friends has to be a decision made by both people. I just want to set correct expectations by letting you know that that outcome may not be achieved.

However, to break up like a great man it's best to just do it! Be honest and clear and do not say things that may lead the girl in a direction that makes her think, "I can get him back." Be very clear on the fact that it is over but you have appreciated and enjoyed your time together. You just feel and think that the relationship has run its course.

One note - do not be her shoulder to cry on. This is where it can get very confusing for women, and for men. When you break up, you cannot be there for her to cry to or to talk to about you. She needs to access her support system and that system cannot be you. That is where you have to be strong; even if you want to listen to her because you care, you cannot. It is misleading and hurts her more in the end.

Marni

How Do Women Evaluate the Men Who Approach Them?
Email:

Hi Marni,

My name is Scott. I just turned 37 in mid-July.

The biggest thing I am trying to understand about women is what sort of criteria women tend to use as a guy approaches them to determine whether she is going to give him a chance rather than writing him off before, he even opens his mouth.

I really have no idea how to even choose approach and open with a woman to get past the initial 15 seconds where physical appearance makes the impression.

I'm in decent shape, but I'm just scared to death of being shot down constantly because of my birthmark and my inability to choose suitable women to approach and get past that initial moment of contact.

Any form of assistance you can provide would be greatly appreciated.

Thanks,

Scott Marks

My response:

Hey Scott,

Totally get where you are coming from with that question. Please know that women evaluate on many levels when selecting men. It is very different from men. Therefore many things come into play: How he looks, how he feels, what he is

To access FREE bonus materials go to:
http://winggirldatingtips.com/gih-bonuses/

wearing (image), what he says, what he does not say, how he presents himself, his character, is he funny etc.

As you can see, it is a big list.

Now, I am not going to lie to you. Having this birthmark on your face can make things a little tougher on you if you do not have anything else for a woman to evaluate you on. Nevertheless, hopefully you do, and judging from your email below, you do.

Some women are going to be superficial, some are going to judge, but the best thing that you can do is say, "Fuck it," approach, and go after any woman you want. If you have this attitude, it will be difficult for a woman not to say the same thing back, "Fuck it, let's see what this guy is all about."

Therefore, for you, I want you to apply the same mentality to your birthmark. I have it and I like it!

Marni

Why Do Women Give Out Their Number & Not Answer the Phone?

You are at a bar talking to a girl you really like and think, "She's totally into me. I'm going to ask for her number."

You: Can I get your number so we can hang out again sometime?

Her: Sure.

You: Great. I will give you a call.

You go home all pumped up, excited, patting yourself on the back. Then two days later, you call.

No answer.

Of course, you try it again because with modern technology, wires are crossed and messages are erased.

Still no answer...

Then you think, "What the hell is wrong with women?" Why do they do this? Why do they give out their phone number and not answer their phone? Do they know this at the time? Or do they decide later?

I have been in the situation many times and the answer is usually I did not intend to ever answer the phone. I was not interested and just being polite. It's easier to say yes to your face and then dodge your calls later.

Women are taught to be proud, polite, respectful ladies. It's not ladylike to hurt your feelings, especially not directly to your face. I know it sounds mean but it's not. Honestly, it's just immature and a little selfish. In that moment, we are not thinking about you; we are thinking how to make it easier on ourselves.

Even knowing what I know now, I still selfishly choose my own comfort over someone else's feelings. It's horrible, I know, but it's what we all do. It is so much easier and less awkward to give out my number then to say, "Sorry I'm so not into you and I will never answer my phone when you call. I do not want to go out with you."

To access FREE bonus materials go to:
http://winggirldatingtips.com/gih-bonuses/

Listen, when I go out I enjoy talking to people. I especially like talking with men but usually within the first two minutes (actually it's more like 30 seconds) I can tell if I am going to want to see a guy past that evening.

However, I still enjoy my conversation with him. Does this mean that I have to cut off the conversation with him? Should I be that presumptuous that he is into me and that I should cut it off before I hurt his feelings?

I usually continue talking because I am enjoying myself and then the awkward moment comes when they ask for my number. I freeze up, get nervous, and give out my phone number feeling guilty the whole time. It's horrible, I know, but it's what I do. It's what all of my girlfriends do and what most women in the world do.

I don't know many women that can be strong enough to say, "You know what, I had a great time with you this evening but I think this is the end of the road for our relationship. It was nice meeting you. Goodbye."

Doesn't happen often.

What I am telling you is that a number does not mean success. The real success is when you actually get that woman to answer the phone and go on a date with you. So what can you do to fight against this? Honestly, nothing. Because no matter what, I want you to always take chances and put yourself out there.

What Does It Mean When a Women Says "You Don't Listen Unless I Yell?"
Email:

This has happened to me twice in five years: A girlfriend gets upset over something and yells at me. I respond by asking, "Why are you yelling at me?" Both girls' response was, "Because you don't listen unless I yell," which is bogus.

My question: What would be a proper response? "That is not true," does not seem to work.

Rob

My response:

The best response is to acknowledge that something is going on that she is worked up about and does not properly know how to express it or state her needs.

- *Take a breath.*

- *Think, "This is about her, not me," so that you can stay calm.*

- *Don't attack or get defensive.*

- *Say to her, "Let's talk about this."*

- *Touch her in some way so that she feels comforted.*

- *If she still is bitchy or pushy, let her know you want to help but it's hard to talk with her when she is all worked up. If she needs a minute alone, you will give her that and then you can talk.*

Marni

VII.   Conclusion

When you wake up tomorrow, how will you feel about yourself? Will you replay a conversation over and over again you had with a woman who rejected you or will you feel amazing knowing that you put yourself out there and walked away with all of your limbs intact?

Listen - there is no perfect formula. I cannot give you a magic line that will get her in bed with you or make you glow when you walk into a room filled with beautiful women; but I can tell you this. Women want a lot more than you have been led to believe.

The Checklist

Here is your checklist:

- Self-assured

- Calm

- Cool

- Collected

- Confident

- Direct

- Leader

Where is rich on the list? Good looking? Muscular? Tall? Not there and for good reason. The successful, gorgeous guy stumbling out of his Porsche in his Prada loafers will be dumped for there is just something boring about him; you can find him any day of the week, and twice at cocktail hour.

My goal with every man I meet - in person, on the phone or through email - is to give him that "something." It's confidence. It's the ability to cater to a woman's raw, primal desires - not the superficial ones TV makes you think she wants. When you hit on the perfect mixture of bravado, kindness and confidence you create a feeling in her that's nearly impossible to describe but that will put you front and center on her radar every time.

Here's the best part, and the one thing I hope you take away from this book - these traits are not handed down by the gods of pick-up lines. They are not genetic and they certainly are not for sale. Any man can have them, if you take the time to turn yourself on and realize that you are the ultimate man for any woman you meet.

The challenge is that you have to want to do it, you have to be dedicated to it, to covet a different demeanor, one that attracts women, and you have to take steps to attain it. The battle of the sexes is just that, a battle. It's not going to be easy, you won't go from John Doe to John Rambo overnight, but through basic training, building skills, endurance, and practice, you will surprise yourself.

To access FREE bonus materials go to:
http://winggirldatingtips.com/gih-bonuses/

The Formula for Success

Let's look at one possible formula for approaching women:

Woman's behavior (variable) + Confidant approach (constant) = my attractiveness as a man (emotional sabotage)

Every woman you meet will be different and even if you throw in a constant of doing the same thing, you still receive different results. Therefore, all you know for sure is that you have already made a decision. You are going out to receive feedback. What you can change is how you feel after the fact.

Use this formula for dating instead:

Your perceived value (constant) + Confidant approach (constant) = my dating opportunities (strengthened resolve)

How do you create a heart-centered connection with someone close to you? I think the best way to do it is to let the other person see you naked. I do not mean this in the physical sense, but in the emotional/spiritual sense. As you converse with the other person, talk about your career; then let it go. Talk about your past; then let it go. Talk about your other relationships; then let those go as well. Keep talking and connecting without re-hashing the same subjects. Eventually you will come upon a thought that is uncomfortable for you to explore. This is where you must summon the courage to delve in and share.

If there is an end goal here, it has to reach the point where you feel so safe with each other, that you can ask absolutely anything and get an emotionally deep and honest answer in response, no matter how embarrassing the questions may seem or how painful the inner wounds are. You become completely naked to each other with nothing left to hide.

In practice, this involves a bit of a dance. Sometimes you will come upon new truths that are too intense or too difficult to face right away. Sometimes you will not feel very connected to your inner truth, so you will not be sure what to say. When that happens, you can back off a bit and discuss something easier and more mundane for a while, or simply take a break. Then later when you feel ready, you can return to exploring the deeper levels of yourselves once again.

As the woman shares herself with you, let her know that she is unconditionally loved and accepted by you. Do not judge her or invalidate her experience. Just keep your heart open, and quietly observe. Making yourself vulnerable by sharing truths about yourself in turn makes it easier for the other person to feel accepted by you because you are giving her the chance to accept you first.

Do not wait — initiate. When in doubt about who should take the next step to reveal something deeply personal, you go first. Prove to life, the universe, and your partner that you are willing to take a risk and that you are willing to trust. Magical things happen when you do that. Emotional risk-taking creates emotional depth.

When you open your heart to someone and share the deepest truths about yourself, and they do the same, you gradually strip away layers of falsehood and self-deception, aligning yourself with ever-deeper truths.

Doing this with someone else creates an amazing sense of connectedness.

To access FREE bonus materials go to:
http://winggirldatingtips.com/gih-bonuses/

It is a life-changing experience to see another human being as she really is and to allow her to see the real you — to see your inner beauty and magnificence reflected back to you in the eyes of another.

The Happily Ever After

Everybody always says that when they finally hear the words "Will you marry me?" it is the happiest moment of their lives. I want to let you in on a secret. It was not exactly like that for me and I do not think it's fair to make you believe it will be for you (as least not for sure but we can hope). I finally received my proposal after five years; I had just heard that my best friend from childhood was mad at me and debating continuing our friendship.

I was also at home visiting my family, who I love with my all my heart, but I moved 5,000 miles away for a reason. When these words were said to me, I honestly did not even hear them. I was off in my own world and had no clue that a proposal was happening right in front of me. My "magic moment" that I had been waiting over five years for was finally happening and I was missing it.

It is not that I was not madly in love with fiancé. It is that I have a problem being present and noticing what is going on around me. Moments like these seem to escape me all the time. It did not hit me that I was engaged until later that evening when I was scarfing down a whole marble cake my mother had made. I was not nervous, or worried. I was happy. In fact, when I went to sleep that night, I woke up ten times, looked at my hand and then giggled to myself.

I was definitely happy. I had finally gotten what I wanted. I was engaged. Cut to two weeks later. My fiancé and I were home in Los Angeles and I started to notice that I was looking at him differently. I was watching him like a hawk and evaluating. I had never done this before. "How will that characteristic play out with our children?" Or, "Does he have to make that noise?" All things that had never crossed my mind in the past.

Then it hit me. I was evaluating whether or not my fiancé was a potential life partner for marriage. Something I should have been doing during our courtship and entire relationship. I was doing what Jordan had been doing our whole relationship, being smart, and thinking about a lifelong commitment. I did not realize until that moment just how focused I had been on getting the person.

I met him when I was 23 (he was 33) and from the beginning of our relationship, I wanted to hear that I was "the one." No need for marriage, just the professions that I was more special than others were. I spent our whole relationship in "why won't he marry me" mode that I forgot to ask myself, "Do I want to marry him?"

Well the next few months were a bit of a roller coaster. Decisions are not my strong suit and the constant questions thrown my own way were driving me crazy. What will that mean for us in the future? I felt like an insane person. I did not know if I was alone in this, so I reached out to a few friends and they told me that they experienced something very similar post-proposal. Some of this questioning even went deep into their marriages.

To access FREE bonus materials go to:
http://winggirldatingtips.com/gih-bonuses/

I did not want these questions to linger past today, let alone to our fifth wedding anniversary. I talked to Jordan about it. I am sure many would have advised against it, but I believe in open communication, in fact that is exactly what I teach the hundreds of thousands of men I coach around the world to do. I sat down and had open communication about what I was going through.

Of course, he was panicked at first but once we got past those ego-hitting moments, we really talked. Talked about everything we should have been talking about: fears, worries, questions, happiness, our idea of partnership and commitment. That conversation was what made me realize that I did want to marry him and he was most certainly the one for me.

Not because he answered everything openly, but because he made me feel secure. It was in that moment that I knew we were a good team. We could overcome things, and that made me happy. Jordan and I have now been married for just a little over two years. He is a great husband and although we still have up and down moments, I know that he is the man that I want to go through each of those moments with.

While marriage may be a long way from your life, do not make the same mistakes I did. Start asking yourself those all-important life questions now. It will help you in situations you never thought possible. From screening the women, to knowing when you find the one, by putting the patience and practice into what you want from life you can enjoy the process a lot more.

Always remember that dating is fun, that you have the option to say no at any time and never take rejection as anything less than a reflection of someone else. Not all people who connect will fall in love; that's what makes it so darned special for those who are willing to look and embrace. Those who find it, look for it!

I wish you every success on your journey!

Marni Kinrys

VIII.   References

Free Bonuses

http://www.winggirlmethod.com/get-insider-her-bonus

The Wing Girl Method

http://www.winggirlmethod.com/

How to Become a Man Women Want

http://www.winggirlmethod.com/how-to-become-the-man-women-want/

Citations

Hazell, A. (2011). How to show confident body language when approaching women.

Retrieved from http://www.winggirlmethod.com/wp-

content/uploads/2011/11/Confident-body-language-with-women.pdf

Karney, B. (Karney, 2012). The relationship institute at UCLA. Retrieved from

http://www.uclarelationshipinstitute.org/d/services_main

Kinrys, M. (2012, January 11). 10 ways to get her in the mood. Retrieved from

http://www.winggirlmethod.com/10-ways-to-get-her-in-the-mood/

Norton, V. (2012, June 05). How to build confidence with women. Retrieved from

http://collectionofconfidence.com/confidencewithwomen/how-to-build-

confidence-with-women/

Rudder, C. (2010, January 10). The four big myths of profile pictures. Retrieved from http://blog.okcupid.com/index.php/the-4-big-myths-of-profile-pictures/

Strauss, N. (Strauss, 2005). The game: Penetrating the secret society of pickup artists. It

Books; First edition. Retrieved from: http://www.amazon.com/Game-

Penetrating-Secret-Society Artists/ dp/0060554738/

ref=la_B001H6NT1I_1_1?ie=UTF8&qid=1354999231&s r=1-1

The art of the approach: The A-game guide to meeting beautiful women [DVD].

(2010). Available from http://www.amazon.com/Art-Approach-Guide-

Meeting-Beautiful/dp/0977650529

Tracey, J. (2011, March 26). Happy guys finish last, says new study on sexual

attractiveness. Retrieved from

http://www.sciencedaily.com/releases/2011/05/1105 24070310.htm

16530800R00166

Printed in Great Britain
by Amazon